TOUR OF THE QUEYRAS

A CIRCULAR WALK IN THE
FRENCH ALPS

GR58

The French Alps

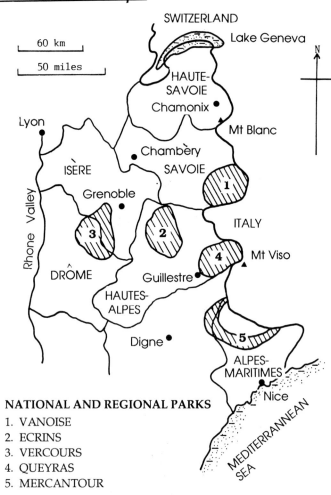

SWITZERLAND
Lake Geneva

60 km
50 miles

N

HAUTE-
SAVOIE

Chamonix

Lyon

Chambèry

ISÈRE   SAVOIE

Grenoble

Mt Blanc

1

ITALY

3   2

4   Mt Viso

DRÔME

Guillestre

HAUTES-
ALPES

5

Digne

ALPES-
MARITIMES

Nice

MEDITERRANNEAN
SEA

NATIONAL AND REGIONAL PARKS

1. VANOISE
2. ECRINS
3. VERCOURS
4. QUEYRAS
5. MERCANTOUR

TOUR OF THE QUEYRAS

A CIRCULAR WALK IN THE FRENCH ALPS
GR58

BY

ALAN CASTLE

CICERONE PRESS
MILNTHORPE, CUMBRIA

ISBN 1 85284 048 X

FOR MY WIFE

"To climb steep hills
Requires slow pace at first."

Shakespeare

Monte Granero, Monte Viso and the Pellice valley

"Regions mountainous and wild, thinly inhabited, and little cultivated, make a great part of earth, and he that has never seen them, must live unacquainted with much of the face of nature, and with one of the great scenes of human existence."

Dr Johnson

ACKNOWLEDGEMENTS

The author would like to thank his wife, Beryl Castle, for all her encouragement during the planning and writing of this guidebook.

Thanks are also due to Andrée Cain for help with the French language.

CONTENTS

Introduction

INTRODUCTION

THE FRENCH ALPS

The French Alps stretch from Lake Geneva (Lac Léman) in the north for some 250 miles (403 km) south, ending at the Mediterranean coast in the vicinity of Nice and Menton. They form a natural frontier with Italy to the east and Switzerland to the north. The weather tends to be warmer and more stable than in the Swiss and Austrian Alps.

The French Alps can be divided into three main regions, *viz.* the Savoie (Savoy), Dauphiné and Provençal Alps. The mountains are to be found within seven 'départements': the Haute-Savoie, Savoie, Isère, Drôme, Hautes-Alpes, Alpes-de-Haute-Provence and Alpes-Maritimes (see diagram). Of these the Isère and the Drôme contain mainly the lower massifs or Pre-Alpes. Possibly the most impressive region of the Pre-Alpes is the Vercours, west of Grenoble and now a Regional Park. The Chablis Alps south of Geneva are rich in lush, green alpine pasture that borders onto Switzerland. This area leads to the major summits of the Northern French Alps, culminating in Mont Blanc at 15,759ft (4,807m), the highest peak in Western Europe. Here also are the other great mountains of the French Alps: Grandes Jorasses (13,795ft/4,208m) Aiguille du Midi (12,595ft/3,842m) and Aiguille Verte (13,513ft/4,122m). South of Chamonix and the Mont Blanc region is the Vanoise, a National Park. Here are many glaciers and high peaks, including the well known La Grande Casse (12,638ft/3,855m). South-west of the Vanoise is another National Park, the Ecrins. The major summits of the Ecrins, La Meije (13,054ft/3,982m), Mont Pelvoux (12,936ft/3,946m) and the Barre des Ecrins (13,447ft/4,102m) are all seen to advantage on this Tour of the Queyras. The Queyras region itself lies to the south-east of the Ecrins, in what is generally considered to be the northernmost part of the Southern French Alps. Further south lies the newest of the French National Parks, the Mercantour. Summers here tend to be hot, and the mountains rather arid, as the Alps finally run out at the Côte d'Azur.

In common with the other mountain regions of Europe, the French

Alps have suffered from depopulation since the Second World War. Today the major industry is tourism and during the winter months skiing is an important source of income. There is still plenty of non-intensive farming and forestry is also much in evidence. Employment is also available in the hydro-electric industry and in the management of the National and Regional Parks.

THE QUEYRAS

The Queyras is a rather isolated region of the French Alps, situated in the eastern half of the département of the Hautes-Alpes, bordering Italy on three sides. Turin lies to the east in a wide valley at the foot of the Piedmont Alps. The Queyras lies within the old province of Dauphiné, having been part of France since 1349. The correct pronunciation of 'Queyras' is a little unclear. Remember that in French 'qu' is pronounced rather like a 'k'. Locals often do not pronounce the 's', whereas most French people who live outside the region pronounce the word with the final consonant.

The major peaks of the Queyras (Pic de Rochebrune: 10,884ft/3,320m; Grand Glaiza: 10,795ft/3,293m; Le Pain de Sucre: 10,517ft/3,208m; Tête des Toillies: 10,409ft/3,175m; Le Grand Queyras: 10,209ft/3,114m; Bric Bouchet: 9,825ft/2,997m; Tête du Pelvas: 9,602ft/2,929m) are lower than than those in the Vanoise to the north and the Ecrins to the north-west. There are no glaciers in the Queyras which is ideal hillwalking country with several of the mountain summits attainable by the ordinary walker without the use of specialist equipment or skills. The region is scenically of the highest order and because of its location there are first-rate views of the neighbouring summits of the Ecrins and of the Piedmont Alps in Italy.

The main geographical feature of the Queyras is the Guil Valley. The River Guil rises high up in the mountains on the border with Italy in the Monte Viso region. It flows first to the north-west, passing La Monta and Abriès, before turning to the south-west, passing Aiguilles, to Château-Queyras. From here the river continues below the hamlet of Bramousse to enter the deep Combe de Queyras before flowing into the River Durance near the fortified town of Montdauphin. The

River Guil is met on several occasions during this Tour of the Queyras.

The major town of the Queyras is Guillestre, on the south-western outskirts of the district. There are several large villages or small towns in the region which have expanded over the last decade to accommodate the growing skiing and tourist industry (e.g. Abriès, Saint-Véran, Ceillac). The nearest large town to the Queyras is Briançon, 21 miles (34 km) north of Guillestre on the N 94 along the Durance Valley.

The classic road approach to the Queyras is via the famous Col d'Izoard (7,740ft/2,361m) on the D 902 from Briancon and Cervières. This is one of the most impressive road passes in the Alps, providing spectacular views for the tourist, but is usually made impassable by snow from October to May. The other approach is from Gap to Embrun to the south-west, through the Combe de Queyras on the D 902 to Château-Queyras and on up the Guil Valley to Abriès. The mountains effectively prevent a southern approach to the region and the peaks and high cols forming the Franco-Italian border isolate the district from Italy. There is one route through the heart of the Queyras and over into Italy that runs from Château-Queyras to Ville-Vieille, then on past the Demoiselle Coiffée (a natural feature which consists of a high earth pillar surmounted by a large boulder) to La Rua, Molines-en-Queyras, Pierre Grosse, Fontgillarde and up to Col Agnel on the border with Italy. However, the latter stages of this ascent are only served by an unsurfaced track, requiring the use of a four-wheel drive vehicle. Surveyors were at work on this track in September 1988 and it is possible that it will be surfaced to link up with the metalled road descending from Col Agnel to Chianale in Italy, and so on to Turin. This route is an ancient one and many scholars believe it to be the line taken by Hannibal and his elephants in the legendary crossing of the Alps. There are several cul-de-sac roads in the Queyras which allow tourists and others to admire the scenery. The road up the Cervières Valley to Les Fonds is one example. Other examples include the road to the Belvédère du Viso in the Upper Guil Valley and the road along the Mélezet Valley from Ceillac to La Riaille.

The Queyras, like most other regions of the Alps, has experienced depopulation over the last 150 years on account of the hardships of rural mountain life and the effects of two world wars. The Queyras, being so close to Italy, suffered considerably in the last war and was the scene of much mountain warfare (witness the destruction of La Monta and Ristolas in the Upper Guil Valley). The population of the Queyras stood at around 8,000 in the mid-nineteenth century, but today the resident population is much lower than this. For example, Molines-en-Queyras had over 1,000 inhabitants in 1838 but this had declined to 290 by the mid-1970's. However, skiing and tourism have now helped to stabilise the population.

The typical architecture in the Queyras has houses built half of stone and half of wood, with high hay lofts or 'greniers'. Many of these were built in the 17th and 18th centuries. There are good examples to be seen in La Rua near Molines-en-Queyras and in Saint-Véran and Aiguilles.

The Catholic religion has always been strong in the Queyras and ample evidence of this will be seen on the walk in the numerous shrines, chapels, ornate churches and 'carpenter's crosses'. There was considerable religious intolerance here in earlier centuries leading to the emigration of many Protestants to the more religiously tolerant German states in the north.

The Queyras is famous for its honey (miel) and numerous hives will be seen whilst on the walk. It is now a minor tourist industry. Wood carving is another speciality of the region. Plenty of examples of local handicrafts will be seen in the village shops and hamlets along this Tour of the Queyras.

Further information on places to visit in the Queyras and events and activities in the region will be provided by the local tourist offices (Syndicat d'Initiative, Maison du Tourisme or Office de Tourisme). There are tourist offices in Guillestre, Ceillac, Saint-Véran, Molines-en-Queyras, Abriès, Aiguilles, Château-Queyras and Arvieux.

WALKING IN THE FRENCH ALPS

Many people in Britain are under the impression that the Alps can only be explored by the experienced mountaineer or Alpinist, or that these mountains are the playground of the package-tour skier. In fact there are many well trodden and clearly waymarked paths beneath the permanent snowline that thread through the valleys, ascend to the high cols and traverse the ridges. These paths are used by young and old alike and there has been a tradition amongst the people of Central Western Europe, who live far from the seaside, to take their family holidays amongst these mountains. Therefore British hillwalkers or ramblers should not consider the Alps to be beyond them. If they can manage a walking holiday in the English Lake District or in the Highlands of Scotland, then an Alpine tour should be within their capabilities. Indeed many of the Alpine trails are easier to negotiate than the rough, often pathless terrain of the Highlands where there are few waymarks and Arctic-like conditions, even during the summer months, frequently occur.

There are, however, certain differences between walking in the Alps and in the mountains of the British Isles. Firstly, the Alps are at a considerably higher altitude: in Britain one is used to thinking in terms of 3,000-4,000ft for the major peaks, in the Alps this figure is 3,000-4,000 metres, i.e. over three times that size. The highest point reached on this Tour of the Queyras is 10,517ft (3,208m) on the Pain de Sucre, and even the lowest col is at 7,379ft (2,251m) above sea level (the Col de Bramousse). As very few people are affected by altitudes below about 10,000ft (3,050m), it is usually only above this height that altitude sickness and associated problems are experienced, there is generally no cause for concern in spending a holiday at these quite modest altitudes. Furthermore, although heights of 9,000ft (2,950m) and above are regularly attained on this walking tour, it must be remembered that in the Alps even the major valley systems are at a significantly higher altitude than those in Britain. The village of Saint-Véran, for instance, at 6,622ft (2,020m) is over twice the height of Scafell Pike, the highest mountain in England. Hence the total amount of climbing in any one day is often no more than in the Welsh,

English or Scottish mountains.

The mountains of the Alps rise steeply out of the valleys and climbs therefore often tend to be longer and more sustained than those in Britain. However, in many cases the ascent of a very steep mountainside is made relatively easy by the construction of numerous zig-zags to take the well made path high into the hills. For example, on this Tour of the Queyras the ascent to the Col des Thures (Day 9) is greatly facilitated by a seemingly endless zig-zagging path.

In most of the mountain areas of Britain, the nearest valley can usually be reached from the highest hills within 2-3 hours. The scale of the Alpine mountains, however, means that it is often not possible to travel on foot from one mountain base to another within one day. To overcome this problem an elaborate network of mountain refuges has been developed, offering comfortable, albeit spartan accommodation in the most isolated areas of the mountains. These refuges are very popular and a tradition of travelling in these mountains, making use of this type of accomodation is well established. There is no equivalent system in Britain and so the British hillwalker on a first visit to the Alps will find the mountain refuges a novel and hopefully enjoyable experience.

The French Alps, particularly those to the south of the country in the Hautes-Alpes and the Alpes-de-Haute-Provence, tend to enjoy warmer and more settled weather than the Swiss or Austrian Alps. This can present problems during the main summer months for the unwary walker who is unused to climbing steep mountainsides under the intense heat of a southern midsummer sun. Heat exhaustion and dehydration are not problems often encountered on the British hills, but they are not uncommon in the warm French Alps. Common sense and an appreciation of the danger is all that is usually necessary.

Walking in the French Alps, then, is well within the capabilities of the average British hillwalker. This section has been included to encourage the potential first-timer as this particular tour is ideal for those contemplating their first walking trip in foreign mountains. The majority of walkers will return many times subsequently!

A word of warning must nevertheless be given, for the Alps have claimed many thousands of lives over the years. They are large scale mountains with plenty of natural hazards and although the weather tends to be generally good in the Queyras, severe weather conditions can and do occur, often with very little warning. An eye to the weather and care when placing one's feet should always be exercised. Most of the paths on this Tour of the Queyras are, under normal conditions, without any special problems, although some of the routes (particularly those on some of the optional excursions such as Le Pain de Sucre, Monte Granero and Tête du Pelvas) are very steep and should only be attempted by those with sufficient experience.

GRANDES RANDONNEES

France has a very extensive network of long-distance paths called Grandes Randonnées (literally, Big Walks), commonly abbreviated to GR. Each GR route has been designated a number e.g. GR 7, GR 20, etc. The principal long-distance trails carry a low number (e.g. GR 4/ GR 5) whilst shorter, circular routes, variations or link routes have two or three digit numbers. Trails in a particular area, or in the vicinity of a single digit GR route, all carry the same first number. For example, the major GR trail in the French Alps is the GR 5 (part of the 1,294 miles/2,083 km European E 2 route from Holland to Nice) which enters the Alps at Lake Geneva and continues south to the Mediterranean. The Alpine part of the GR 5 is also known as La Grande Traversée des Alpes and is the subject of another Cicerone guidebook (see Appendix 4). There are several other GR paths in the French Alps and these all carry the same first number, viz. 5, so that the Tour de L'Oisans for example is numbered as the GR 54 (and covered by yet another Cicerone guide, see Appendix 4).

Other GR routes in the Alps include the GR 52 (a variation of the GR 5 from Saint Dalmas-Valdeblore to Menton through the Mercantour National Park) and the GR 58 (Tour du Queyras) which forms the basis of the walk described in this guidebook. GR routes which are circular walks are generally referred to as tours.

There are also a few 3 digit GR trails in the Alps which again carry the same initial number and are often link routes to the longer trails.

For instance the GR 541 links the GR 54 in the Ecrins to the GR 58 in the Queyras. This system has analogies with the road numbering system in Britain - M6, M62, etc. There are at present some 25,000 miles (40,250 km) of GR trail throughout France. In addition there are regional footpaths, GR de Pays, and Sentiers de PR (Petite Randonnée) which are short local footpaths. In all there are some hundred thousand miles of country footpaths in France.

Italy also has its long-distance trails. The major Alpine route is the Grande Traversata delle Alpi, an alternative to the French Grande Traversée. Rather confusingly these are both abbreviated to GTA. The Italian traverse runs from Carnino in the south, across the Argentera massif, skirting the Monte Viso region, to the Gran Paradiso and on to end at the foot of Monte Rosa at Macugnaga near to the Swiss border.

A second Italian trail of relevance to the Queyras Tour is the circular Tour of Monte Viso ('Monviso' in Italian). This commences at the Pian del Re, the source of the River Po, and circles the peak of Monte Viso and adjacent mountains. The route, which takes 3/4 days to complete, goes from the Pian del Re to the Rifugio Quintino Sella (for an optional and very long ascent to Monte Viso), then over the Passo di San Chiaffredo to enter the Vallone di Vallanta (in French, Valante). The trail climbs in this valley, passing the refuges of Gagliardone and Vallanta, to join the route described in this guidebook. The tour crosses the Passo di Vallanta (in French Col Valante) to enter France and descends to the Refuge Baillif-Viso. Soon after this the Monte Viso Trail parts company with the Queyras Tour to cross back to Italy at the Colle de la Traversette and descends back to the Pian del Re.

WALKING TOUR OF THE QUEYRAS (GR 58 AND GR 541)

The walking tour of the Queyras described in this guidebook (and henceforth referred to as the Tour) makes use of two GR trails and their variants, as well as a number of non GR footpaths. The two GR routes are the GR 58 (Tour du Queyras) and the GR 541.

The standard GR 58 is a circular tour from Ceillac—> Saint-

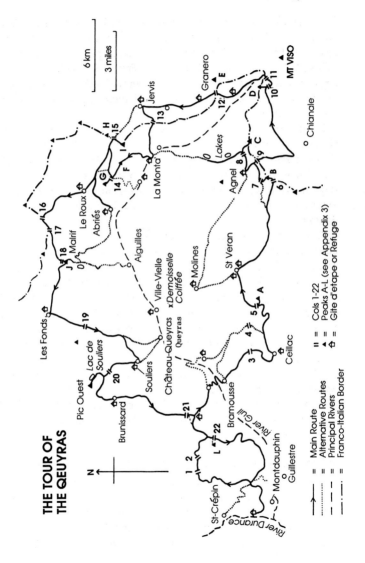

THE TOUR OF
THE QEUYRAS

→ = Main Route
--- = Alternative Routes
--- = Principal Rivers
-·-· = Franco-Italian Border

|| = Cols 1-22
▲ = Peaks A-L (see Appendix 3)
⌂ = Gîte d'etape or Refuge

Véran—> Refuge Agnel—> Col Vieux—> Lac Foréant—> Lac Egourgéou—> La Monta—> Ristolas—> Abriès—> Lac du Grand Laus—> Col du Malrif—> Les Fonds de Cervières—> Souliers—> Brunissard—> Furfande—> Les Escoyères—> Ceillac. There are two alternative routes from Les Escoyères to Ceillac, both referred to as the GR 58, one via the Col de Bramousse and the other via Montbardon and Col Fromage. The standard route of the GR 58 lies entirely within France.

There are also four official alternative routes (variants) to sections of the standard GR 58. These are all on the eastern or northern sections of the route. Two of them include sections within Italy. The variants are as follows:

GR 58A

From Abriès to Souliers via the Lac du Grand Laus, Aiguilles, Chalvet and Les Meyriès. A relatively low-level variant (except for the climb to the Lac du Grand Laus) but one which involves considerable ascent, descent and re-ascent before joining the standard GR 58 route before Souliers. This variant is not used on the Tour.

GR 58B

From L'Echalp in the Upper Guil Valley to Abriès via Italy. The route enters Italy at Col Lacroix and descends to the Rifugio Jervis at Ciabot del Pra. The return into France is made via the Col d'Urine. The Tour in this book uses part of this route.

GR 58C

From the Refuge Agnel to La Monta via two excursions into Italy. This major two-day variant is from Refuge Agnel—> Col Agnel—> Soustra Valley—> Passo della Losetta—> Col Valante—> Refuge Baillif-Viso—> Col Sellière—> Pellice Valley—> Ciabot del Pra—> Col Lacroix—> La Monta. A small section of the route is co-incident with the Italian Tour of Monte Viso. This variant is walked in its entirety in the Tour described in this guidebook.

GR 58D

From La Monta to Les Fonds de Cervières. This is a relatively new variant and has been dubbed 'the high mountain alternative.' The route is from La Monta—> Sommet de la Lauzière—> Collette de

Gilly—> Le Roux—> Col des Thures—> Col de Rasis—> Col du Malrif—> Les Fonds de Cervières. The whole route of this variant is included in this Tour. These four official variants have been detailed here in case reference is made to these routes on signpost or map. Note that these variants are waymarked in the same manner as the standard GR route (see Waymarking and Navigation).

The GR 541 is a long-distance trail linking the GR 54 (Tour de L'Oisans) in the Ecrins with the GR 58 in the Queyras. The two great massifs are separated by the wide and deep Durance Valley in which is situated the town of Briançon. This valley carries the main-line railway from Gap to Briançon and also one of the major routes nationales, the N 94. About half of the GR 541 is followed in the Tour described in this book, namely the eastern section from the Durance Valley into the heart of the Queyras and Furfande. Not only is this a fine route in itself, but it also allows the walk to be started straight from a main-line railway station, without further travel arrangements. There are two routes from the Durance Valley to Furfande; the standard GR 541 and the GR 541 variant. The latter, which is used in the ascent to Furfande, crosses two high cols and passes a mountain lake and is scenically the finer of the two routes. The standard GR 541 is used in the final descent of the holiday.

The walking Tour described in this guidebook includes most of the standard GR 58 and a large proportion of the major variants described above. Minor variants are taken occasionally (e.g. to the Col de Saint-Véran and the Pic de Caramantran on Day 4) where the route and scenery are preferable to the standard trail. The various optional and alternative routes are all described. All of these trails are clearly marked on the Didier and Richard and IGN maps. In addition the Tour described includes a number of optional ascents of mountain summits that are passed on the way, but which are not part of any official GR route. In all the Tour crosses twenty-one cols and provides optional ascents of twelve peaks (see Appendix 3). There is therefore plenty of variety from woodland glades to rocky high-level cols, from Alpine pasture to airy summit. The Tour includes two excursions into the Italian Alps and there is plenty of opportunity to shorten or

19

lengthen the route as time and conditions dictate. The walk is ideal for those new to Alpine walking, whilst providing optional challenges for the more experienced. Most of the Day stages are not over-long, allowing plenty of time for admiring the magnificent scenery or attempting an additional summit or footpath. Time is available at the end of a two-week holiday to visit Guillestre and nearby Briançon.

CLIMATE - WHEN TO GO

The Queyras enjoys one of the best climates of all the Alpine regions. There are approximately 300 sunny days per year and very often the mountains lie under a clear blue sky with uninterrupted views. Hill fog occurs less frequently than it does further north. Summers are warm but, because of the high altitude of the valleys and villages, they rarely become uncomfortably hot. Rainfall is relatively low. However, low cloud and violent storms can occur in these mountains at any time of the year and the walker should be well prepared. The air temperature can change very rapidly in the Alps at altitude: it can snow above about 8,000ft (2,440m) during any season although for the most part sunny, warm, settled weather is the general pattern through the summer months. The area does not suffer from the very hot and dry conditions experienced further south towards the Mediterranean. The combination of landscape and climate make the Queyras an ideal area for high mountain walking.

Snow remains on the high passes usually until June and even into early July in some years. The heavy winter snows return any time from mid-October onwards. Hence the season for the summer hillwalker lasts from about mid-June until the end of September. Only the experienced and equipped mountaineer or cross-country skier should venture on this route between November and May. Many of the gîtes d'étape and refuges do not open until mid-June (see Appendix 1). The majority of the French take their holidays between the 14th July (Bastille Day) and the 15th August (Assumption); gîtes d'étape, refuges and hotels are likely to be very crowded during this period. The second half of August and the first half of September are possibly the best periods to go walking in these mountains. Snow is by then usually absent from even the highest cols and peaks, the weather tends to be warm, sunny and fairly settled and the gîtes d'étape and refuges have relatively few guests but still remain open. After the first or second week of September some of the gîtes and refuges close for the year (see Appendix 1). Hence if travelling after the first week of September it is advisable to carry a small tent, although in some cases a closed refuge will have a permanently open shelter attached (e.g. Refuge de Furfande). Finally, those who wish to see the best of the Alpine flowers should go towards the end of June when the Queyras is covered with them.

TRAVELLING TO THE QUEYRAS

There are four possible means of travelling to the Queyras from Britain, by air, train, coach or private transport. Note that any timetable information and prices given are liable to change. When consulting timetables remember that France is one hour ahead of Britain for most of the year (liable to change).

AIR

Five destinations are worthy of consideration. British Airways and Air France are the principal carriers.

Lyon

There is a daily service from London Heathrow to Lyon. A bus service operates between the airport and Lyon city centre (bus departs approx. every 20-30 minutes all day Monday-Friday, but mornings only on Saturday, Sunday and Bank Holidays; the bus fare is about 35FF one way). Alternatively a taxi from the airport will cost about 150-180FF (1990 prices).

From Lyon take the main-line train to Montdauphin-Guillestre. Note that in Lyon there are two main-line stations, *viz.* Lyon-Perrache and Lyon-Port-Dieu. There is a night train from Lyon-Perrache direct to Montdauphin-Guillestre (depart approx. 02.25, arriving approx. 07.46). During the daytime it is usually necessary to change at Valence. There are several daily trains from either Lyon-Perrache or Lyon-Port-Dieu to Valence with a journey time of about 1 hour. (Note that a more frequent service operates from Lyon-Perrache than from the other station.) From Valence take the train going to Briançon via Gap. There are several such trains each day and they all stop at Montdauphin-Guillestre, journey time approximately 3 hours 15 minutes.

Geneva

There are several daily flights from Heathrow, Gatwick and Manchester airports to Geneva in Switzerland. Flying time is about 1 hour 30 minutes. There are also charter flights operating from Gatwick to Geneva throughout the year. Remember that a quantity of Swiss currency will be required if travelling to Geneva. There are both bus and train services available between Geneva airport and town (distance 2 miles; journey time approx. 15 minutes). From Geneva there are two possible routes to the Queyras:

(1) By train to Grenoble (several trains daily). From here take the bus (VFD) to Briançon. The bus station (gare routière) is adjacent to the railway station at Grenoble (turn left on leaving the railway station). The bus to Briançon runs twice daily (usually 08.40 and 16.55 from Grenoble; the journey time is approx. 3 hours 15 minutes). The bus terminates at the railway station at Briançon. From here take the train to Montdauphin-Guillestre (several trains per day; journey time approx. 30 minutes).

(2) Take the train to Lyon-Perrache and continue the journey as described under 'Lyon' above.

Turin

There are daily flights from Heathrow to Turin (Torino) in Italy. Some Italian currency will be required. A bus service operates between the airport and the city centre. From Turin take a bus to Briançon and from there the train to Montdauphin-Guillestre.

Nice

There are several daily scheduled flights from Heathrow and Gatwick to Nice. There are direct flights from Manchester to Nice on Saturdays and Sundays. Moreover, charter flights operate from Gatwick and from Manchester to Nice during the summer months. A regular bus service runs between the airport and the town (approx. price 15FF, distance 4 miles, journey time about 20 minutes). From Nice there are two possible routes to the Queyras:

(1) Take a bus via Digne and Gap to Guillestre (enquire at the bus station in Nice for details).

(2) Take a train to Valence (approx. journey time 4 hours 30 minutes to 5 hours 30 minutes; trains daily). From Valence take the train to Montdauphin-Guillestre as described under 'Lyon' above.

Paris

Several flights per day operate between London (Heathrow and Gatwick) and Paris (Charles de Gaulle). Flying time is approximately 1 hour. Scheduled services are also operated from Birmingham, Glasgow and Manchester. Charles de Gaulle International Airport is approximately 15 miles from Paris city centre (journey time approx. 45 minutes). There are three possible modes of transport between airport and city: Air France bus (fare 34FF), Roissy Rail train (fare 30FF) or taxi (fare 150FF) (1990 prices).

Once in Paris the Paris-Briançon main-line train can be taken to Montdauphin-Guillestre (see below).

TRAIN

The train is possibly the best form of public transport to and from the Queyras region of France. Indeed the walking itinerary of the Tour of the Queyras described in this guidebook starts and finishes at a main-line railway station (Montdauphin-Guillestre) which is on a direct line to Paris.

French Railways (SNCF - Société Nationale de Chemins de Fer) provide a first-rate service throughout the country. Trains are not expensive and generally fast, punctual, clean and comfortable. The journey to the Queyras from Britain is via Paris and so there is an opportunity to spend a day or more in the capital before continuing the journey to the Alps.

There are two principal ways in which the train can be used to travel to the Queyras:

(1) **Train and cross-channel ferry to Paris, followed by train to Montdauphin-Guillestre.**

It is possible to reach the Queyras from London in about 22 hours using train and cross-channel ferry. The journey can be considered in three parts.

(a) *London to Paris*

There are several trains between London and Paris operating daily during the day and night on two principal routes:

(i) London, Victoria—> Dover or Folkstone—> Calais or Boulogne—> Amiens—> Paris, Gare du Nord (journey time approx. 7 hours).

(ii) London, Victoria—> Newhaven—> Dieppe—> Rouen—> Paris, Gare Saint-Lazare (journey time approx. 9 hours).

Route ii involves a longer channel crossing (about three hours forty-five minutes) than Route i (about one hour forty-five minutes). There is also a nightly service from London, Waterloo to Paris via Portsmouth and Le Havre (journey time approx. 10 hours). Note that cut-price fares often operate between London and Paris but there will usually be no reduction for a journey from Dover or Newhaven to Paris. Indeed it may cost more for a ticket from these channel ports to Paris than from London to Paris! Therefore, if making independent travel arrangements to Dover or Newhaven, it is best to purchase a ticket from London to Paris and disregard the first part of the ticket to the channel ports. However, these things often change, so check first before buying your ticket.

(b) *Across Paris*

Trains from Britain arrive in Paris at either Gare Saint-Lazare or Gare du Nord. It will be necessary to cross Paris to the Gare de Lyon for trains to the Queyras. The easiest way of travelling across the capital (other than taxi) is to make use of the métro (Underground) system. Simply ask for one ticket. There is no need to state the station to which one is travelling as there is a fixed price whatever the destination. Note that if spending some time in Paris, it is more economical to buy a 'carnet' of 10 métro tickets. Crossing Paris can be somewhat of a hassle, particularly if unsure of the system, so it is a good idea to write down the following brief instructions on a small piece of paper that can be kept in the pocket and discarded later. Armed with this it will be unnecessary to consult métro maps at stations.

(1)   From Gare du Nord to Gare de Lyon: Line 5 (Direction Place d'Italie) to Bastille (7 stops). Change to Line 1 (Direction Château de Vincennes) to Gare de Lyon (1 stop).

(2)   From Gare Saint-Lazare to Gare de Lyon: Line 12 (Direction Mairie d'Issy) to Concorde (2 stops). Change to Line 1 (Direction Château de Vincennes) to Gare de Lyon (8 stops).

On the return journey:

(1)   From Gare de Lyon to Gare du Nord: Line 1 (Direction Pont de Neuilly) to Bastille (1 stop). Change to Line 5 (Direction Bobigny-Pablo Picasso) to Gare du Nord (7 stops).

(2)   From Gare de Lyon to Gare Saint-Lazare: Line 1 (Direction Pont de Neuilly) to Concorde (8 stops). Change to Line 12 (Direction Porte de la Chapelle) to Gare Saint-Lazare (2 stops).

The journey time is approximately 30 minutes, although it is wise to allow at least an hour (preferably two) between main-line trains arriving from London and departing to the Alps. Small maps of the métro system (and also the bus and RER services) can be obtained free of charge at métro stations. Ask for a 'Petit Plan de Paris.'

Note that a few main-line trains (SNCF) operate between Gare du Nord and the Gare de Lyon, although they are not often convenient.

(c)   *Paris to the Queyras*

From Paris, Gare de Lyon catch a train going to Briançon. The journey is via Lyon and Valence. Alight at Montdauphin-Guillestre, two stops before Briançon. The journey time varies between 7-11 hours, depending upon the train taken. The overnight train (departing Gare de Lyon at about 21.17) is direct and arrives at Montdauphin-Guillestre at 07.46. Couchettes are available on this train (supplement payable). It is thus possible to start the Tour directly from the Montdauphin-Guillestre railway station having had a night's sleep on the train from Paris. There are several trains during the daytime which are generally faster than the night service but usually require a change, often at Dijon or Valence. Small blue timetables ('horaires') can be obtained at main-line stations (e.g. at Gare de Lyon), these give the current trains operating between Paris and Briançon. Timetable no. 525 (Paris-Briançon) is the relevant sheet.

(2) **Airplane to Paris and Train from Paris to Montdauphin-Guillestre.**

This is possibly the best combination of air and train travel. The somewhat lengthy and unpleasant channel crossing is avoided and the train from Paris is both fast and convenient for the start of the walk. Details of the two stages of the journey have been given in the relevant sections above. Air France and SNCF offer combined air and rail tickets at very reasonable prices, i.e. air to Paris and train from there to one's destination (e.g. London to Briançon, return £119).

General Information about Train Travel in France
Booking
Travel Centres at major British Rail stations in most large cities in the UK can supply timetable and price information. They can also book tickets and make seat and couchette reservations. A seat/couchette reservation is advisable if travelling during the peak holiday season (particularly at weekends). However, note that SNCF reservations will only be accepted within two months of your travel date.

It is not absolutely necessary to book tickets in Britain for the whole journey: for example, if staying for a short while in Paris before travelling to the Alps, more flexibility will be available if a ticket to the Queyras is purchased at the Gare de Lyon prior to departure. The same is true for the return journey. Buying a train ticket at a railway station in France is no more difficult than in Britain. However, there are two problems with this option, *viz.* all the seats on the train may already have been booked (this is a particular problem in main season at weekends), and if one's French is poor, then the wrong ticket may be bought! A ticket purchased in Britain is valid for two months from the date of outward travel. A ticket bought at a railway station in France is valid for two months from the date of purchase. Tickets can be used on any trains, although on certain services (see below) a supplement may be payable. Seat and couchette reservations are extra.

Types of Trains

The French are justly proud of their train service and boast that 1,400 express trains run every day throughout France. Many of the services on the Paris to Briançon run are express trains and some are special trains, such as the air-conditioned Corail Trains. The pride of French Railways is the TGV (Train à Grand Vitesse) which travels up to an incredible 168mph. A supplement is payable on this service, which operates between Paris and Lyon and Paris and Grenoble and can thus be of use to the passenger wishing to continue to the Queyras. The Paris-Lyon run takes only 2 hours!

All express trains have some form of catering, from a simple 'mini-bar' pushed by an attendant passing through the train, to a lavish restaurant car on the TGVs.

Couchettes are equipped with bed linen, pillows and blankets. there are 6 berths per compartment in 2nd class and 4 berths per compartment in 1st class.

Types of Ticket

There are several types of 'saver' ticket available on French railways which save you up to 50% off the normal fare:

(1) Frances Vacances Pass: this provides unlimited 1st or 2nd class rail travel throughout France on any 4 days during a period of 15 days or on any 9 days during a period of 1 month.

(2) Holiday Return (Sejour) ticket: 25% reduction on a return or circular journey of at least 1,000 kms.

(3) Rail Europ Family (REF) card: this costs £5 at the present time. With it one member of a family pays full fare whilst all the others qualify for up to a 50% reduction on rail travel and up to 30% reduction on channel crossings.

(4) Rail Europ Senior (RES) card: this is available to those over 60 who are holders of a BR Senior Citizen Railcard. A RES card holder is entitled up to a 50% discount on rail travel and up to 30% reduction on channel crossings.

(5) For those under 26, Inter-rail cards and Carte Jeune are both available.

Further details can be obtained from major BR Travel Centres and from most railway stations in France. Note also that there is an English language train information service in Paris. This can be dialled on 45.82.08.41.

One cautionary note. Access to railway station platforms is free in France, but tickets must be validated by date stamp before boarding the train. This simple task is performed using the orange-coloured machines which are located on the concourse of nearly all French railway stations. Failure to do so can result in a fine.

COACH

Probably the cheapest way of reaching the Queyras is by long-distance coach. Eurolines operate a number of services to France from Victoria Coach Station in London. Bookings can be made, and further information obtained, from principal National Express offices and agents throughout Britain. The services of interest are as follows:

(1) *London to Grenoble*

A service operates during the main summer season on Mondays, Wednesdays, Fridays and Saturdays which leaves London at 15.00 and arrives at Grenoble at 09.00 the following day. From Grenoble a bus can be taken to Briançon (see under AIR, Geneva), then from there a train to Montdauphin-Guillestre.

(2) *London to Lyon or Turin*

During the summer season a coach leaves London at 21.30 on Sundays, Wednesdays and Fridays bound for Lyon (arrival time 14.30 the following day). This continues via the Frejus Tunnel to Turin in Italy (arrival time 22.00). The Queyras can be reached from either Lyon or Turin as described under AIR above.

(3) *London to Paris*

An inexpensive coach service operates between the two capitals several times a day. This could be used to reach Paris, from where a train could be taken to the Alps.

All of these coach services are direct and luggage deposited in the coach at the start of the journey need not be retrieved until the destination has been reached (with the exception of carrying one's luggage through British Customs on returning to the UK). Several stops are often made en route, but the London-Paris run is non-stop.

The British Mountaineering Council also organises a non-stop coach from London to Grenoble during the main summer season. Details from the BMC (see Appendix 5).

PRIVATE TRANSPORT

The disadvantage of driving a car to the Queyras is that it will have to be parked for the duration of the Tour. Sometimes a car can be left in a hotel car park, provided that a night or two is spent in the hotel at the start and finish of the trip.

From the UK drive across France to Grenoble. There are two routes from here to Montdauphin. The fastest and easiest route, although the longest (149 miles/240 km), is from Grenoble to Gap on the Route Napoléon (N 85) and then on to Embrun and Montdauphin on the N 94. The direct and more scenic route is along the N 91 via Bourg d'Oisans, La Grave, the Col de Lautaret and Le Monêtier-les-Bains to Briançon. This route gives an opportunity to view the mountains of the Ecrins at close quarters. From Briançon drive down the Durance Valley on the N 94 to Montdauphin. If additional time is available, it is worth driving on the D 902 over the Col d'Izoard (7,737ft/2,360m), one of the most impressive road passes in Europe. This route is usually closed by snow from October to June. Continue via Brunissard to Guillestre and Montdauphin.

It is useful to understand the road classification in France. Motorways (autoroutes or A roads) are toll roads. Although fast, it is fairly expensive to travel across the country by autoroute. The speed limit on autoroutes is 130 km/hr (81mph). N or RN roads (routes nationales) are roughly equivalent to British A roads. D (département) roads are equivalent to British B and C roads. The speed limit on dual carriageways is 110 km/hr (68mph) and 90 km/hr (57mph) on single carriageways. In built-up areas the speed limit is 60 km/hr (36mph) unless otherwise indicated. Radar speed traps operate in France and the French police can inflict on-the-spot fines. Seat-belts are compulsory as in Britain. It is advisable to carry a red warning triangle in case of accident or puncture and to obtain a Green Card level of insurance.

LOCAL TRANSPORT
Public transport within the Queyras is reasonable for an Alpine region. There is a main-line train service (SNCF) which operates along the Durance Valley from Briançon to Embrun and beyond. Buses reach several parts of the Queyras including Guillestre, Ceillac, Château-Queyras and Abriès. (Full details of train and bus services are given in Appendix 2.) Taxi services are available at the Montdauphin-Guillestre railway station and in several of the villages and towns. If all else fails, try hitch-hiking; the locals are aware of the difficulties of travel in these mountain areas and you are quite likely to be given a lift.

OVERNIGHT ACCOMMODATION
There are basically two ways of tackling this Tour: either making use of gîte d'étape, refuge or hotel accommodation overnight; or backpacking the route carrying tent, stove and cooking utensils. Although it is perfectly feasible to backpack in the French Alps, the author believes that on this particular Tour it is better to make use of permanent overnight accommodation. The latter is particularly recommended for those going to the Alps for the first time, or for walkers unused to carrying heavy loads. There is an abundance of good, cheap accommodation at regular intervals along the route and it is never necessary to walk long distances to reach a night's lodgings. Furthermore, virtually all of the gîtes d'étape and refuges provide breakfast and dinner at reasonable prices and so food need only be carried for lunches and daytime snacks. Alternatively, all of the gîtes d'étape and some of the refuges have fully equipped kitchens where one's own food can be prepared and eaten.

The backpacker, although carrying an extra burden, has greater freedom and the possibility of spending idyllic nights camping out in the high mountains. A tent and associated equipment will be necessary for those walkers visiting the area either early or late in the summer season when some of the gîtes d'étape and refuges are closed (see

Appendix 1). Backpacking can of course provide a cheaper holiday than gîte or refuge 'hopping', but only if the necessary equipment is already owned!

MOUNTAIN REFUGES

Walking and climbing in the European Alps is facilitated by a network of mountain huts. The term 'Alpine hut' is hardly apt for these mountain refuges, some of which are elaborate buildings. Most of the mountain huts in the Alps are owned and operated by the Alpine club of the country in which the hut is situated. In France this is the Club Alpin Français (CAF), in Italy the Club Alpin Italiano (CAI). A few of the refuges in the Queyras (e.g. Furfande and Agnel) are run by the GTA, the same organisation that operates the extensive network of gîtes d'étape.

Whereas gîtes d'étape tend to be located in villages or small towns, mountain refuges are usually, but not always (e.g. Agnel), situated in isolated areas of the mountains well away from metalled roads. They are usually built to serve a particular need, such as to provide a base for climbing a particular group of mountains or a stopover for hillwalkers on long-distance trails. Mountain huts ('refuge' in French and 'rifugio' in Italian) as well as gîtes d'étape are marked on both IGN and Didier and Richard maps. A few establishments are, however, unsure of their category (e.g. the building at Les Fonds de Cervières is marked as a gîte d'étape on the maps, but refers to itself as a refuge).

Refuges are usually substantial buildings of stone and/or wood with unisex dormitories, a kitchen/dining room/sitting room and toilets. All the refuges on this Tour have a resident guardian during the summer months and it is important that, on arrival, a bed space is booked immediately. It is not often possible to book in advance and places are allocated on a first come, first served basis.

During the main season the most popular refuges can become very crowded, but it is very unusual for a late arrival at a full refuge to be turned away, although it may be necessary to sleep on the floor. Many refuges now have their own generator, although the guardian is often reluctant to allow electric lights to be used for very long in the evenings. The general rule is to go to bed when the sun sets and to get up fairly early in the morning. In those huts which cater primarily for climbers (there are none of these on this Tour), the hut comes alive in the dark of the early hours of the morning as the Alpinists prepare to make their ascent on the peaks before the sun has softened the snow too much and made conditions dangerous. Some people greatly enjoy the atmosphere in a mountain refuge, whilst others prefer the peace and quiet of a tent. Whatever your feelings about moutain refuges they are sure to provide a novel experience.

The overnight fee in the refuges owned by the GTA (Furfande and Agnel) is similar to that for the gîtes d'étape (*q.v.*) . However CAF (Baillif-Viso) and CAI refuges (Granero and Jervis) are somewhat more expensive (60FF in CAF refuges and 10,000 lira in CAI rifugios in 1989). However, discounts are available in CAF and CAI refuges to holders of a Reciprocal Rights Card, or for members of one of the European Alpine clubs. These discounts are quite considerable: in 1989 the reduced rate for card holders was 30FF (50% reduction) in CAF refuges and 7,000 lira (30% reduction) in CAI refuges. This saving has to be balanced against the cost of a Reciprocal Rights Card or the membership fee of an Alpine club (both are renewable annually). In 1989 the fee for a Reciprocal Rights Card, obtainable from the British Mountaineering Council (see Appendix 5), was £14. As the walker on this Tour is only likely to spend one night in a CAF refuge (or possibly up to two more in CAI refuges), it is not worth purchasing a Reciprocal Rights Card or applying for membership of an Alpine club unless several other stopovers are planned in Alpine refuges during the same calendar year. Note that no discount is offered in GTA refuges.

Meals are provided at all of the refuges used on the Tour. However, if you go self-catering it will be necessary to carry a stove and cooking utensils as this equipment is not always provided in refuges. Hot water is seldom available and any shower provided is likely to be connected to a cold water source!

The majority of mountain refuges are only open with a resident guardian during the summer months, although several (e.g. Agnel)

Château-Queyras (Day 10 - optional excursion)

Saint-Véran (Day 3/4)

have a second high season during the winter, providing accommodation for skiers and winter mountaineers. When the main refuge is closed (commonly from mid-September onwards), there will usually be a small annex or 'winter room' left permanently open to provide shelter and overnight accommodation. The facilities available here will be fairly basic.

New gîtes d'étape and refuges are sometimes opened (such as the new gîte d'étape at Ristolas which was opened in the summer of 1988), whilst occasionally an establishment will close down. Sometimes a gîte or refuge will close down earlier than usual in the season and perhaps open up later than is common. It is a good idea to become aware of the current situation. Information about neighbouring gîtes d'étape and refuges is often posted up in the gîtes; alternatively, ask the guardian if there are any new establishments along the next section of the trail. A couple of months before leaving for France it might be a good idea to write to CIMES (see Appendix 5) who will supply the latest information on all gîtes d'étape and refuges in the French Alps. Be sure to enclose an International Reply Coupon. The latest edition of *Gîtes d'étape de Randonnée et Refuges* by A & S Mouraret is a very useful source of information (see Appendix 4). As a final note, however, it should be stressed that most of the gîtes and refuges used as overnight accommodation on this Tour are well established and are unlikely to close, at least in the foreseeable future.

GITES D'ETAPE

There are several thousand of these simple hostels found all over France, particularly along the GR trails. They provide basic and cheap accommodation for the outdoor enthusiast, especially the walker. Gîtes d'étape form the basis of the overnight accommodation on this Tour. If the itinerary described in this guidebook is strictly followed, then 8 or 9 out of the 13 or 14 nights will be spent in gîtes d'étape.

Gîtes d'étape come in all shapes and sizes, from converted barns or stables to large houses or parts of hotels. Few are purpose-built. The guardians are often farming folk who use the gîte d'étape as an extra source of income. The typical gîte d'étape will accommodate between

10 and 30 people in a unisex dormitory, usually on large mattresses. Its kitchens will be equipped with stoves and cooking utensils and there will also be a dining area. There are usually hot showers as well as washbasins and toilets. The guardian often does not reside in the gîte d'étape but may live in an adjacent house or farm. Meals are often provided by the guardian and these generally represent good value for money.

Many of the gîtes d'étape in the Queyras, as in other parts of the French Alps, have been established by an organisation known as the GTA (Grande Traversée des Alpes). However, it is not necessary to be a member of any organisation to spend the night at their gîtes d'étape. No discount is offered to members of any clubs or associations. Gîtes d'étape provide inexpensive accommodation and there is usually a standard rate for all GTA gîtes d'étape. In 1988 the overnight fee in the gîtes d'étape on the Tour varied between 30-35FF (about £3-£3.50).

Gîtes d'étape are primarily intended for walkers travelling along the GR trails and, under normal circumstances, one is not encouraged to stay any longer than a few days at any one gîte. They do, however, make ideal bases in which to sit out a spell of bad weather and tend to be better for this purpose than mountain refuges as many of them are situated in villages or small towns and so there are often shops and other facilities available. Sometimes a small fee is payable for use of the gîte during the daytime. Gîtes d'étape can become very crowded on occasions and, although the guardian will seek to accommodate everyone, late arrivals may have to go elsewhere. If there is nowhere else to go within reason, then it is most unlikely that entry will be refused, however full the gîte. It is possible to book ahead by telephone, but good spoken French is necessary for this as few guardians speak English. Overcrowded gîtes d'étape are most frequently encountered between mid-July and mid-August. Arriving early at a gîte d'étape is the best way of reserving a bed for the night. Remember also that dinner is usually served some time between 7-8.00 p.m. at most gîtes and refuges; a late arrival will therefore go hungry if not carrying his or her own provisions.

HOTELS

Some walkers may prefer to spend some nights whilst on the Tour in hotels which will provide privacy and comfort. Hotel rooms are available at the following locations:

(1) Near to the Montdauphin-Guillestre railway station
(2) Montdauphin
(3) Guillestre
(4) Saint-Crépin
(5) Ceillac
(6) Saint-Véran
(7) Ristolas
(8) Abriès
(9) Le Roux
(10) Aiguilles
(11) Arvieux.

Hotels in France are star-graded on a system very similar to that in use in Britain. The basic hotel is the one-star establishment and this is usually reasonably priced, clean and comfortable. A list of hotels can usually be obtained from the local Syndicat d'Initiative or Maison de Tourisme.

Sometimes hotels or restaurants have associated outbuildings or attics. These 'dortoirs' provide basic, but cheap accommodation for the night. Some villages, whilst not boasting an hotel, may have an 'auberge', a simpler sort of establishment often with rooms above a café/restaurant.

CAMPING

It is perfectly possible to backpack on this Tour and camp wild each night. Such a trip will provide some memorable pitches in superb locations. There are certain areas (e.g. Furfande) where wild camping (camping sauvage) is not allowed; the fine for disobeying this rule is considerable. Elsewhere it is generally acceptable to camp wild provided that a site is chosen above the valleys and well away from habitation and roads. The art of the backpacker is to leave no sign of an overnight camp. Leave no litter and take care not to pollute water sources. Particular care should be exercised with matches and stoves; forest fires are all too common in the hot, dry summers. Do not light open fires.

There are limited opportunities for staying in official campsites on this Tour. There is a campsite adjacent to the Gîte d'Etape d'Eygliers and several others in the vicinity of Guillestre (Days 1 and 13). On Day 2 there is a campsite in the Mélezet Valley, some 1.25 miles/2 km south-east of Ceillac.

Although camping is extremely popular in France, tents tend to be of the large frame variety and the French have not taken enthusiastically to backpacking. Therefore a small backpacking tent will often be squeezed in between large family tents. It will be necessary to provide passport details and complete a registration form. Many campsites in France are extremely well equipped having bars, restaurants, sports facilities, hot showers etc. However, large family groups often make a lot of late night noise!

EATING OUT

France is, of course, renowned for its cuisine and one of the delights of a walking holiday in the French Alps is the opportunity to eat out at several different establishments. Most restaurants have a range of fixed-price menus as well as à la carte. Fixed-price menus in most restaurants in the French Alps range from 50FF to approximately 120FF (approx. £5 to £12). The average meal costs around 60-80FF: for this price there is usually a choice of hors d'oeuvre, a main course (usually a meat or fish dish) and sweet, fruit and/or cheese. Wine is generally extra, but is of course much cheaper than in Britain. The 120FF menu would probably be a five or six course affair. It is a good idea to finish the holiday with such a meal as a celebration. Eating out in restaurants in France is, in general, cheaper than in Britain and the choice of establishments is much greater. The smallest village will often have one or more restaurants and even in the most isolated and rural parts of the country one can expect food of high quality at reasonable cost. Many restaurants in France are hotel-restaurants, but almost always meals are available to non-residents. Quite often a restaurant will double as a café or bar and will serve drinks and snacks to customers not requiring a meal.

There are a few differences between eating out in France compared with Britain that should be appreciated. Firstly, the menus for lunch and dinner are usually the same (i.e. lunch is a large meal in France). Most walkers will prefer to eat their large meal of the day in the evening, but occasionally it might be appropriate to walk in the morning and evening and escape the heat of the day in a restaurant over a long, slow lunch. Note, however, that a snack at lunchtime can often cost as much as a full meal! Dinner is not normally available until 7-7.30 p.m. Breakfasts are "continental," consisting only of coffee (or drinking chocolate) with bread and jam (average cost 15-20FF in 1988). Lastly, one small point; the same knife and fork are generally used for most courses on the menu so do not expect to get a clean knife and fork with every course.

Nearly all of the gîtes d'étape and refuges on the Tour provide meals. Dinner and breakfast are usually always available and a few establishments also serve lunch. Meals in the gîtes d'étape are generally of the same quality and price as in a restaurant. Indeed some gîtes d'étape (e.g. La Monta, Les Fonds de Cervières, Brunissard) are also restaurants which accept non-resident customers. In the refuges (particularly those belonging to CAF and CAI) meals tend to be slightly more expensive and at times the quality is not so high. However this is only a generalisation; the author has had many first-class meals in Alpine huts.

Finally, of the gîtes d'étape and refuges used as overnight accommodation on this Tour, the author would particularly recommend the meals provided by the following establishments: Refuge Agnel, La Monta, Les Fonds de Cervières and Brunissard. Remember that this is a personal choice, that different guardians take over refuges and gîtes from time to time and that the quality of meals provided is therefore liable to change.

FOOD

Grocers and other food shops are to be found in the following locations on the route of the Tour:

(1) Near to the Montdauphin-Guillestre railway station

      (Days 1 and 13)

(2) Ceillac   (Day 2)

(3) Saint-Véran (Day 3)

(4) Abriès   (Day 9)

(5) Brunissard (Day 11)

There are also food shops in Guillestre, Molines-en-Queyras, Chianale, Ristolas, Aiguilles, Arvieux and Château-Queyras, all of which can be reached by detour from the standard Tour. There are a few other possibilities for buying food, either en route or after a short detour, and these are mentioned in the relevant place in the text. Where mention is made of a shop in this book it is always a reference to a shop where food may be purchased, unless otherwise stated.

A supermarket is a 'supermarché'; a grocers' shop is an 'épicerie' or 'alimentation'; bread is sold in a 'boulangerie' or 'dépôt de pain'; cakes, pastries and biscuits are sold in a 'patisserie' and cold meats, sausages and pâté in a 'charcuterie'. These shops tend to open earlier than their equivalents in Britain (usually around 7.30-8.00 a.m.) and stay open later (often up to 8.00 p.m.). The disadvantage is that they close for much longer during the lunch hour'. A walker arriving in a village any time between noon and 3.30 p.m. is likely to find the shops closed. Provisions can sometimes be purchased from the guardian of a gîte d'étape and this is particularly useful when there is no shop in the immediate vicinity.

Dehydrated meals are difficult to obtain in rural France and therefore, if desired, should be purchased in Britain before leaving for the Alps. However, French packet soups are very good and a wide variety of them is on sale everywhere; when supplemented with pasta or biscottes' and perhaps saucisson sec and cheese, they can provide a tasty, basic meal. Fruit, vegetables, cheese, cold meats and sausages are excellent and widely available. Milk is usually of the UHT variety and sold by the litre in disposable containers. The commonest form of bread is the baguette which, although tasty, will become very stale within a few hours. Longer lasting wholemeal bread is becoming more readily available in France and this is generally more suitable on a walking holiday. Pain d'épice (spiced 'bread') is widely available and makes a tasty, anytime snack.

WATER
Water sources are found fairly frequently on this Tour and lack of water should not prove a problem on most stages. There are water fountains in many of the villages and hamlets and water bottles should always be filled when the opportunity arises. Temperatures during the daytime can become very high at times, particularly during July and August, and heat exhaustion and dehydration can rapidly develop when carrying a pack on steep mountainsides. Always ensure that an adequate quantity of liquid is consumed.

Most of the water sources are safe to drink from, but of course one can never be sure, particularly if there are cattle, sheep or goats in the vicinity. If in doubt add a water purifying tablet to any unboiled water, allowing at least 10 minutes for the chemicals to react before drinking the water. Water labelled 'L'eau non potable' is not suitable for drinking.

EQUIPMENT
A lightweight sleeping bag is essential for the backpacker and highly recommended for those walkers making use of gîte d'étape and refuge accommodation. Not all gîtes d'étape, and few of the refuges, supply blankets. Most walkers find a 3/4 season sack to be unnecessary for much of the time in these southerly latitudes, although it can sometimes be fairly cold at altitude at night, even during the height of summer.

For much of the time shorts and T-shirt will be the most comfortable attire, but warm clothing should be carried to allow for possible deterioration in the weather and for evening use. A waterproof and windproof jacket is essential and many people would also wish to carry waterproof trousers. A pair of thin gloves weigh very little and could save discomfort if the weather turns cold at altitude. Rather than carry the heavy weight of traditional breeches, it may be preferred to pack a pair of lightweight walking trousers which can be worn on the occasional cool day or to protect sensitive skin against sunburn. Such trousers can also be worn whilst relaxing in the evenings.

The glare and heat from the sun can be intense, particularly during July and August and at altitude. The use of a sun-hat, high factor sun-cream and lip-salve will all help to avoid over exposure to the sun. Sunglasses may also be useful. To ensure that fluid is readily available during the day, at least one 1-litre bottle should be carried per person. Mineral water is often sold in screw-cap plastic bottles in France and these can provide useful additional water carriers.

Well worn-in boots are essential for this walk. Some type of lightweight shoe is also desirable for rest days and for relaxing in the evening and for sightseeing. A pair of good quality trainers is recommended as these can be used as an alternative form of footwear on easy sections of the route. Note that, in general, one is not allowed to wear boots inside refuges and gîtes d'étape.

A small first-aid kit is important as there will only be the occasional opportunity to buy simple medicines en route. Include plasters, antiseptic cream, safety pins, a small bandage, aspirin/paracetamol and anti-diarrhoea tablets. Insect repellent may also be useful. The first-aid box is a good place to store a whistle as it can then be located easily in an emergency.

There are several miscellaneous items that may be of use. A small torch is invaluable in navigating a route across a sea of slumbering bodies in a crowded refuge. A small French/English dictionary or phrasebook may help with communication. A small Swiss army knife or similar implement will provide a sharp blade for cutting (e.g. bread, salami), a pair of scissors, a can opener and a corkscrew. A small, lightweight pair of binoculars is one luxury item that most people will greatly appreciate in this scenic mountain country. Binoculars are also useful for observing the wildlife (e.g. marmots, chamois).

The rucksack is probably the most important item to be carried. It is vital to inspect the sack thoroughly for wear before leaving for

France. Try to ensure that the carrying mechanism is not likely to break whilst on holiday. Apart from injury, this is the worst fate that can befall the walker, particularly in an area such as the Queyras where the possibility of repair or replacement is remote. A dustbin liner for the rucksack and a supply of plastic bags should keep equipment dry in heavy rain. Equipment is best packed in different coloured stuff sacks to enable easy identification and access: the author generally uses one stuff sack for spare clothes, one for kitchen equipment and one for maps, guidebooks, writing paper etc. Perishable food is best kept in a disposable plastic bag to prevent the accidental soiling of the inside of the rucksack.

The backpacker will need to carry additional equipment, with a small lightweight tent the main requirement. A closed-cell type of insulating mat will cut down loss of body heat through the ground. A stove will be necessary, and probably the most convenient to use in France during the summer months is the camping gaz variety (spare gaz canisters are easily obtainable in France at several of the villages on the tour). Methylated spirits (alcool à brûler) and lead-free petrol can also be purchased in France. If travelling by air it is important to remember that none of these fuels can be carried on board an aircraft, they will have to be purchased on arrival. A small cooking set will also be required, but if carrying a Swiss army knife or similar, then the only item of cutlery really needed is a spoon. Don't forget a box of matches or a lighter!

A rope will not be required on this Tour. Similarly, neither ice-axe nor crampons should be necessary during the summer months, although the possibility of freak weather covering the high passes with snow and ice can never be ruled out. Note that in some years snow and ice can be late in clearing from some of the high passes; outside the main summer months an ice-axe and crampons are essential items of equipment.

MAPS

(1) Didier and Richard 1:50,000

Sheet No.10 (Massifs du Queyras and Haute Ubaye) covers the entire route of the Tour and also includes the Durance Valley up to Briancon. All the hiking trails, including the GR 58, GR 541, GR 5 and their variants, are clearly marked on this map. Recommended.

(2) IGN 1:25,000 (Serie Bleue)

Three maps are required to cover the complete Tour described in this guidebook:

(i) Sheet No.3637 Ouest (Aiguilles, Parc Naturel Régional du Queyras).

(ii) Sheet No.3537 Est (Ceillac, Château-Queyras, Parc Naturel Régional du Queyras).

These two sheets cover the entire route except for the first few miles at the start and end of the walk (i.e. the route to the Lac du Lauzet on Day 1 and the section west of Gros on Day 13 are excluded). Walkers intending to omit the GR 541 and GR 541 variant from their itinerary would only require these two sheets. To complete the full Tour of the following sheet is also required:

(iii) Sheet No.3537 Ouest (Guillestre).

The 1:25,000 IGN maps are of excellent quality and are highly recommended.

(3) IGN 1:50,000 (Serie Orange)

Sheets No.3537 (Guillestre) and 3637 (Aiguilles) are required to cover the whole route. The Didier and Richard map at 1:50,000 is a much better buy.

Note that IGN is the abbreviation for the Institut Géographique National, the French equivalent of the Ordnance survey. All of these maps can be purchased from certain specialist map shops in Britain (see Appendix 5).

WAYMARKING AND NAVIGATION

Mountain trails in Europe are generally waymarked more thoroughly than the mountain paths of Britain. Most of the footpaths used in this

Tour are part of the GR network and as such are waymarked with a system of red and white painted stripes. These occur, usually in a horizontal position with white above red, on rocks, boulders, trees, posts, fences, telegraph poles etc. The standard of waymarking in the Queyras is generally very good and most of the paths are distinct and easy to follow. The walker should not continue too far without seeing another red and white waymark. If a waymark is not encountered for some time, it is likely that the wrong path has been taken.

In a few areas the waymarking is not particularly easy to follow. The section between the Col des Thures and Col du Malrif (north of Abriès on Day 9) requires some care to avoid losing the waymarks. Also the waymarking on the Italian side of the border tends at times to be inferior to that in France. In this guide particular care has been given to the route description for those areas where difficulties in following waymarks may be experienced.

In the GR waymarking system various arrangements of red and white lines are used to signify different instructions. When two sets of red/white marks appear together this signifies that a change in direction is imminent. This instruction is also sometimes indicated by the use of curved red and white markings which point towards the new direction to be taken. The painted cross, usually of one red and one white line, is important as it signals that the route is not in that direction and you must go back to pick up the correct trail. Very occasionally a red and white mark bisected by another white line may be seen; this means that the route is a variant of the main GR trail.

Here and there along the trail, markings others than the standard red and white paint stripes will be seen. For example, in places the route is waymarked with yellow stripes in addition to red/white waymarks. On the ascent of Le Pain de Sucre a route is marked in small cream-coloured arrows and crosses. Remember also that *all* GR trails are waymarked with red and white flashes so, in areas where two GR routes meet (e.g. where the GR 5 crosses the GR 58 in Brunissard and in Ceillac) or where a variant of the GR leaves the main route, make sure that the correct trail is followed!

Many of the cols and the high places are marked with a signpost

At the Col de Bramousse (Day 2)

indicating the name of the area and its altitude. In addition, several wooden signposts will be seen indicating the direction and time to the next col or village. These have either been erected by representatives of the GR authorities (often volunteers) or by the local Maison de Tourisme.

Other notices may sometimes be seen. 'Propriété Privée or 'Defense d'Entrer' means that the area is private and entry is forbidden. The sign 'Reserve du Chasse' and Chasse Privée' do not refer to walkers but indicate that hunting rights are reserved for the owner of the land.

It is foolish to rely solely on the waymarking system. A map and compass must always be carried and one's position on the map frequently checked. This will allow a route to be navigated in safety if the waymarks are mislaid. The map can also be used to find the fastest and easiest escape route if the weather deteriorates. Finally the map and compass are invaluable in the identification of neighbouring peaks, lakes and villages. By the end of the trip the walker should have become very familiar with the topography of the Queyras and the surrounding mountain ranges.

LE PARC NATUREL REGIONAL DU QUEYRAS

Despite its large size and abundance of high quality natural scenery, France has only six National Parks. However, there are many more Regional Nature Parks all over the country, from the Ardennes in the north to the Camargue in the south, from the Vosges in the east to Brittany in the west. These Regional Parks are very similar to the National Parks, except for the way in which they are administered. They have all been established in areas of exceptional natural beauty and are regions where commercial exploitation and development is restricted in an effort to conserve the natural environment and protect the native flora and fauna.

The Queyras Regional Park, established in 1977, is one of two Regional Parks in the French Alps (the other being the Parc Naturel Régional du Vercours, west of Grenoble). It encompasses the whole of the Queyras region from the Gorges du Guil in the west to the Tête du Pelvas in the east, from the Col des Thures in the north to Col Giradin in the south. On the eastern side of the Queyras the boundary of the Regional Park is coincident with the Franco-Italian frontier, from the Grand Glaiza in the north to the Tête des Toillies in the south.

The majority of the walking Tour described in this guidebook is within the boundary of the Queyras Regional Park (henceforth referred to as the Park). The route enters the Park just before Col Saint Antoine on Day 1. It then only leaves the Park on three occasions (twice for detours into Italy on Days 6 and 7 and once for the descent to Les Fonds de Cervières on Days 9 and 10), before finally exiting after the hamlet of Gros at the end of the last day of the walk.

WILDLIFE

Everyone who visits these mountains outside the winter months is certain to encounter marmots. These rather cheeky, likeable animals are large brown rodents with a characteristic shrill wolf-whistle used to warn their fellows of advancing potential danger. The marmot of the central European Alps *(Marmota marmota)* weighs about 5-6 kg when fully grown and is a vegetarian. Marmots are social animals, living in colonies which are found up to altitudes of around 9,000ft (2,745m). They live in burrows, one to each family and these often form complex systems penetrating deep into the hillside and having several exits. When alarmed the marmot will give his warning whistle and then head straight for cover in his home burrow. In areas where marmots are most numerous, some care should be exercised to avoid twisting an ankle by putting a foot down a marmot burrow. Marmots will only be seen during the summer months since between October and April they hibernate in their burrows deep beneath the snow.

The other well known species of mammal found in these mountains is the chamois *(Rupicapra rupicapra)*, a type of mountain antelope with short vertical horns hooked back at the tip. Chamois are found in small herds up to about 13,000ft (3,966m). They are extremely agile and sure-footed, moving with great speed over very steep grass and scree-covered hillside when disturbed. They are shy and nervous by nature but, with patience and luck, they may well be spotted on this Tour.

The bouquetin or mountain ibex *(Capra ibex)* is much rarer than chamois. A magnificent beast with its long, curved horns, once seen it is never forgotten. The males are quite large, hefty animals and the species is found at relatively high altitudes, usually over 8,000ft (2,440m).

The mountain hare is another mammal to be found here: during the summer months its fur is brown, but in winter it changes to white for a most effective camouflage.

There are plentiful frogs and toads in these mountains and many lizards will be seen flitting across the hot rocks during the heat of the day. Vipers and other snakes are common in many areas *(q.v.)*, butterflies and grasshoppers are abundant. Beware at times of the occasional less pleasant, biting insect - the cleg in particular!

There are a number of interesting bird species in these Southern Alps, including a variety of finches, choughs (red bills) and alpine choughs (yellow bills), alpine grouse, ptarmigans, ravens and several raptors, including the occasional golden eagle.

SNAKES

Unfortunately vipers or adders are fairly common in the French Alps and a bite, although unlikely to be fatal, would be exceedingly unpleasant and could have serious consequences in the high mountains where help may not be quickly available. Fortunately they are quite secretive animals and likely to detect a walker's presence by vibrations along the ground and take avoiding action. Nevertheless, keep a good lookout for vipers in order to avoid accidentally treading on one. It is a good idea to familiarise oneself with the markings of the European viper (dark green/black in colour with characteristic zig-zag stripes on the upper surface) in order to identify a specimen if seen. The chances are that the Tour will be completed without catching sight of even one of these reptiles.

A bite from a viper can result in considerable bruising, discolouration and swelling of the surrounding area. If bitten, it is necessary to rest, avoid panicing, get medical help as soon as possible and in the meantime try to suck out the venom. It is possible to buy an aspiratory device for this purpose in pharmacies in France. This aspirator consists of a syringe with various sized and shaped attachments which enable venom to be sucked from a wound. It is also possible to purchase a viper venom antidote (antiserum) without prescription in French pharmacies. The application of this requires a self-injection in muscle tissue near the site of injury, but it should only be used in absolute emergencies when medical help cannot be obtained (see also Insurance).

FLORA

The mountains of the Alps have a rich and varied flora which attracts many thousands of amateur botanists and gardeners every spring and summer. The Queyras is situated in the southern part of the Alps where spring tends to come early and winter later than in the more northerly regions of Austria and Switzerland. Hence the area tends to have an abundance of Alpine flowers including a variety of gentians (spring, purple, trumpet and giant yellow), lilies, orchid, crocuses, asters, irises, anemones, pansies and edelweiss. Carline thistles and many varieties of stonecrop will also be encountered. Unfortunately the habit of picking wild flowers is almost as widespread as the harvesting of wild mushrooms and thus several Alpine species are now rare or even extinct.

The number and variety of Alpine plants is dependent on both altitude and latitude. The limit of the tree-line is around 5,000ft (1,525m). Both larch and pinetrees are common. The Queyras is far enough south for its climate to be affected by the Mediterranean and many species are found here at much higher altitudes than is the norm in the Swiss and Austrian Alps. In the lower valleys of the Queyras many Mediterranean species exist, to be replaced by Alpine varieties at higher altitudes. There are in excess of 2,000 plant species to be found in the Queyras; the keen botanist will not be disappointed!

TRAINING
Those who walk regularly in the hills of Britain should experience no great problems on this Alpine Tour. However, if exercise has not been taken for some time, then obviously some programme of training in the months preceding the trip would be sensible. An unfit person would find the walk a great strain and therefore would lose much of the enjoyment of the Tour, both for him/herself and for his/her companions. Before travelling to France it would be advisable to take a few short walks carrying a pack, in order to become accustomed to carrying a load. Even those making exclusive use of gîtes d'étape, refuges and hotels will probably have to carry at least 15lbs of equipment and personal effects. Backpackers will have to carry significantly more.

HEALTH
Perhaps the most common ailment that befalls walkers in foreign climes is stomach upset or diarrhoea. These problems are usually easily treated with the appropriate tablets obtainable from any good pharmacist in France. Remember, however, the pharmacies are several days apart on this Tour and so it is advisable to include a few tablets in a first-aid kit. Rest and light meals often provide the best

cure. Failure to correct stomach upsets can lead to weakness, dehydration and further complications.

Over-exposure to the sun and heat-stroke are other problems to be avoided at all costs. Always wear a sun-hat and if the weather becomes very hot then set off very early in the morning and have a long siesta during the heat of the day. Drink sufficient liquid to prevent dehydration and cover exposed skin unused to a southern sun.

MOUNTAIN SAFETY

The well equipped and well prepared walker who is sufficiently skilled in the use of map and compass should encounter no particular problems on this Tour. Nevertheless these are high mountains and some previous experience of walking in mountain country is advisable before contemplating this walk. However, the majority of the route is suitable for novices to Alpine walking providing that they are reasonably fit and accompanied by an experienced mountain walker.

Although the Queyras enjoys some of the best and most settled weather in all the high Alps, sudden adverse changes in conditions do occur. Always keep an eye open for weather changes and never hesitate to turn back or head for the nearest shelter if conditions deteriorate. Plan ahead, look for possible escape routes to be used in an emergency, never overestimate the physical ability of the party and always carry sufficient reserves of food. Never be afraid to ask the guardians of the refuges or gîtes d'étape for a weather forecast or other advice, they are usually more than willing to oblige. Other walkers, particularly those who are walking the route in the opposite direction, are another good source of information about the state of the path ahead.

It is important that you known the International Distress Signal *viz.* six audible (e.g. whistle) or visual (e.g. torch) signals for one minute followed by a minute's silence. The alarm is then repeated. The answer from a party coming to the rescue is three such signals, followed by a minute's pause. Help can also be summoned by using arm signals: raising both arms in the air means 'I require assistance'.

One arm raised and the other lowered means 'I do not need help'. In the French Alps, as in other European mountains, it is only advisable to summon the rescue services if it is absolutely essential. It is an extremely costly business (see Insurance).

Finally a warning should be given on the dangers of wet schist in these mountains. There is an abundance of loose and fragmented schist in certain areas. Although fairly safe under dry conditions, it can be very dangerous after heavy rain when it becomes very loose. It is all too easy to slip in these conditions and even cause a landslip of thick, wet schist and rocks. There are few areas where this is a problem on the Tour, but particular care should be exercised in the following regions during or after heavy rain:

(1) The descent from the Col de Chamoussière   (Day 4)
(2) The ascent/descent of Le Pain de Sucre   (Day 5)
(3) Final part of the ascent to the Passo della Losetta and the balcony path from this pass to Col Valante   (Day 6)
(4) The first part of the descent from Col Sellière   (Day 7)
(5) Ascent of the Tête du Pelvas (Day 8)
(6) The section from the Col de Rasis to the Col du Malrif   (Day 9)
(7) The initial part of the descent from the Pic du Malrif   (Day 9).

Schist is much less of a problem in the Queyras than it can be in certain other regions of the French Alps, e.g. the Ecrins.

PHOTOGRAPHY

Most walkers will wish to have a photographic record of their journey through the Queyras. The best type of camera to take is probably the 35mm SLR. The use of a wide-angle lens (e.g. 28 or 35mm) is particularly recommended for the type of landscape photography possible in these mountains. A telephoto lens will be useful for capturing details of more distant features. All of this camera equipment is unfortunately very heavy, but a compromise would be to use a medium zoom lens (e.g. 28-80mm) on a SLR body. This would also obviate the need to change lenses continually, but nevertheless zoom lenses are themselves heavier than prime lenses. Weight can be radically reduced by using a good quality 35mm compact camera equipped with a reasonably wide-angled lens, or alternatively a zoom lens. The quality can be almost as good as an SLR camera, but the compact camera is light and small, easily fitting into a pocket.

It is best to purchase all the film required at home before leaving for the Alps. For colour transparencies either 64 or 25 ASA film is suitable, and for colour prints 100 ASA will yield good results. The use of a UV filter is recommended to cancel the blue bias that UV light has on colour film (light at altitude has a strong UV content). Protect both used and unused film from heat by placing it well inside the rucksack. Finally, it is better to take all exposed film home rather than posting it back to Britain to be processed. It could be lost in the post or damaged by X-ray equipment in the sorting offices.

LANGUAGE

The French, like the British, are not particularly keen on learning foreign languages. Many of the younger people can speak some English, but in general do not expect the level of fluency found in Holland or Germany. It is a good idea to brush up on rusty French before the holiday; even the most elementary grasp of the language will pay dividends by enriching the experience of walking in France. However, no true adventurer will be discouraged by an inability to speak the local tongue, even if it will necessitate the occasional use of sign language!

The Tour takes in part of the Italian Alps and so a few words of Italian might be useful. In the author's experience the Italians generally speak better English than the French, although many of them have less knowledge of French, despite the fact that French and Italian are both major romance languages. However, the French possibly have an even poorer grasp of Italian!

MONEY/BANKS

The major currency required on this Tour is the French franc (approximately 10FF to £1 sterling). Two days are spent over the border in Italy, but if the itinerary suggested in this guidebook is followed strictly, then all overnight accommodation will be in France. Even if a night or two is spent in Italy in one of the CAI refuges, meals and accommodation can usually be paid for with French francs, although do not expect a particularly favourable exchange rate. Therefore it is not really necessary to change money into Italian lira.

It is advisable to carry a fairly large supply of moderately low denomination notes (50, 100 and 200 FF notes are particularly useful). Besides cash, Eurocheques, traveller's cheques and credit cards are all widely used in France. The author has found that Eurocheques are particularly useful, the only problem being that a minimum quantity will have to be exchanged (1,200FF in 1988). French franc traveller's cheques are the most useful as they can sometimes be used in restaurants, hotels, etc. as immediate payment. Access and Visa cards are accepted widely in France and are a useful form of payment for restaurant meals and rail tickets. However, it is likely that few of the establishments along the Tour will accept this form of payment.

There are banks in Guillestre and Briançon. However, the only bank encountered en route is in Abriès (Day 8) and even this town is a slight detour from the standard itinerary. It is therefore essential to carry sufficient currency from the outset in order to avoid a time-consuming and frustrating detour to reach a bank. Normal banking hours are from around 9.00 a.m. until midday and from 2-3.00 p.m. until 4-5.00p.m. Many banks are closed all day Saturday and some of the banks in the smaller towns and villages are only open on one or a few days per week. Occasionally one opens just for a couple of hours each week!

The larger post offices (PTT) in the towns and cities in France will cash Eurocheques. There are post offices in a few of the villages and towns en route (e.g. Ceillac and Abriès) but in most cases these are the equivalent of British sub-post offices and do not have the facilities for cashing Eurocheques.

INSURANCE

It is advisable to take out travel and medical insurance for the duration of the holiday as rescue and hospitalisation charges are very expensive. Ensure that the policy has an adequate medical sum insured and that the costs of mountain rescue are included. The latter should include the use of a helicopter to lift the injured walker off the mountain. In the Alps the hire of a helicopter for such a purpose is extremely expensive (current rates can be as high as £10 per minute!). Several companies issue cover within Europe for hillwalking, rambling, scrambling and camping, i.e. activities excluding the use of specialist equipment such as ropes and ice-axes. Such a policy would be suitable for this Tour, provided that it is taken during the summer season when the mountains are not covered in snow and ice (see Appendix 5).

There are certain reciprocal rights available for British subjects in France and Italy under the National Health Service arrangements within the EEC. Information concerning eligibility for medical cover under this scheme and the necessary E111 form can be obtained from local DHSS offices. It is, however, not advisable to rely solely on a E111 form.

TO TELEPHONE BRITAIN

It is becoming increasingly difficult for the visitor to make a simple phone call in France due to the widespread introduction by French Telecom of the phonecard system. During 1987/8 most of the public telephone boxes in France were converted from payphones to those requiring a phonecard. In Paris it is now almost impossible to find a public cash payphone, the one exception being in the foyer of Gare Saint-Lazare (there is normally a long queue!). During the summer of 1988 most of the Alpine villages in the Queyras had coin-operated public telephone boxes. How long these will remain is a matter for conjecture. Phonecards can be purchased from most post offices and certain other advertised outlets. The price (December 1988) was 40FF for 50 units or 96FF for 120 units. The only alternative is to use a phone in an hotel, café or restaurant, but it is very likely that a call made in this way will be much more expensive than in a public telephone box. The old style 'jeton', or token system no longer operates in France.

The procedure for placing a call to Britain is very simple. Lift the receiver and insert the appropriate coins or phonecard, after which the dialling tone will be heard. The French have had a digital exchange system for many years now. First dial 19 (the code for an international line) and pause until a second dialling tone is heard. Next dial 44 (the code for the UK). Pause again before dialling the STD code of the number required, but minus the initial zero. Lastly dial the number of the line required. For example, to phone a number in Liverpool (STD code 051) dial 19, pause, 44, pause 51 123 4567.

PUBLIC HOLIDAYS

There are more public holidays in France than in Britain. Fortunately between June and October there are only two to consider, Bastille Day on July 14th and the Fête of the Assumption on August 15th. On both of these days the public transport system is considerably affected and many shops are closed, although most cafés and restaurants stay open. It is well to bear these days in mind and to plan accordingly, particularly if it is necessary to travel by public transport on either of these days. In addition do not forget the public holidays in Britain which are different from those in France if you are planning to leave or enter the UK on those days.

For most of the year French time is one hour ahead of the time in Britain (i.e. French summer time is one hour ahead of BST). For a few weeks in late September and early October Britain and France are on the same time (liable to change).

SUGGESTIONS FOR WALKING HOLIDAYS OF VARYING LENGTH AND DIFFICULTY

The 13-day Tour outlined in this guide would make an ideal fortnight's holiday for the average hillwalker, providing a thorough exploration of the Queyras and the neighbouring Italian Alps and allowing for the ascent of several peaks in the area. However, some people will have less time available whilst others, who may not have tried this type of walking before, may want to omit the more arduous and difficult sections of the route. The more experienced hillwalker and scrambler may wish to include as many summits as possible. There is scope for all in the Queyras. Some suggestions are given below for variations on the standard 13-day Tour to suit various categories of walker. There are of course several other combinations of routes and these can be combined with general sightseeing as desired. There is sufficient information in this guidebook to allow other variations to be planned and followed. Several other alternatives are suggested in the text.

One Week Holiday
Bus from Montdauphin-Guillestre railway station to Ceillac.

1st Day:	Ceillac to Saint-Véran.
2nd Day:	Saint-Véran to La Monta via Col Vieux and Lac Egourgéou.
3rd Day:	La Monta to Abriès or Le Roux.
4th Day:	Abriès or Le Roux to Les Fonds de Cervières (either route).
5th Day:	Les Fonds to Brunissard via Souliers, but omitting the Lac de Souliers and Pic Ouest.
6th Day:	Brunissard to Furfande.
7th Day:	Furfande to Ceillac.

The first three days could be contracted to two as shown below.

1st Day:	Ceillac to Saint-Véran to Refuge Agnel, omitting the Col de Saint-Véran (long day).
2nd Day:	Refuge Agnel to Col Vieux to La Monta to Abriès or Le Roux (omitting the Sommet de la Lauzière).

The 6th Day is only half a day's walk and strong walkers could combine it with the 7th Day to make a very long final day. Alternatively Ceillac can be reached in about 8 hours from Brunissard on the GR 5, a route involving considerably less total ascent and descent.

The Novice Alpine Walker

The standard 13-day Tour is acceptable for the first-timer in the Alps, with the following reservations:

(1) *Day 1*

The climb out of the Durance Valley to Furfande is a very strenuous start to the holiday. Those unsure of their capabilities may wish to consider one of three alternatives:

>   (a) Taking a taxi from Montdauphin-Guillestre railway station to Le Coin, thereby shortening the stage and saving 900ft (275m) of ascent.
>
>   (b) Starting and finishing the walk at Ceillac (i.e. commencing at Day 3, continuing to Day 12 and finishing with Day 2, thus omitting Days 1 and 13).
>
>   (c) Ascending to Furfande via Col Garnier (i.e. using the route of Day 13 in reverse). This is somewhat less strenuous than the route via the Col de Moussière and Col Saint-Antoine.

(2) *Day 4*

The direct route to the Col de Chamoussière is less tiring than that via the Col de Saint-Véran and the Pic de Caramantran.

(3) *Day 8*

The route from La Monta to the Collette de Gilly via Ristolas is less strenuous than that via the Sommet de la Lauzière.

(4) *Day 9*

The direct route to the Pic and Col du Malrif from Abriès via the Lac du Grand Laus is better defined than that from the Col des Thures. An even easier route (the GR 58A via Aiguilles) omits the Pic and Col du Malrif altogether. However, it would be a great pity to omit Malrif with its superb view; most 'first-timers' should manage it in good conditions.

(5) *Peaks*

The following peaks should be omitted by those unsure of their capabilities on steep rock and scree: Le Pain de Sucre, Pointe Joanne, Monte Granero, Tête du Pelvas and Pic Ouest. Of these Monte Granero and the Tête du Pelvas are the most difficult.

The Peakbagger

Those experienced hillwalkers wishing to attain as many peaks as possible should rearrange Days 7 and 8 as follows:

New Day 7

Refuge Bailiff-Viso to Col Sellière to Rifugio Granero. Leave overnight equipment at the hut and ascend Monte Granero. Return to Rifugio Granero for the night or continue down the valley to Rifugio Jervis.

New Day 8

Ciabot del Pra in a direct ascent to Col d'Urine. From here ascend the Tête du Pelvas and/or La Mait d'Amunt. Continue directly to Abriès or Le Roux, or if time is still available proceed to the Collette de Gilly for the Sommet de Gilly and/or the Sommet de la Lauzière.

The fit and experienced hillwalker/scrambler could even include an ascent of Monte Viso itself on his/her itinerary. The normal route starts from the Rifugio Quintino Sella in Italy (off-route). It is not a particularly difficult ascent, but is very long and arduous (about 6-7 hours from hut to summit).

NOTES ON USING THE GUIDEBOOK

Layout of Guide

The Tour of the Queyras has been divided into 13 stages each of a day's duration. Each Day has been designed so as to terminate at a place where there is overnight accommodation, either in a gîte d'étape or refuge or, occasionally, the possibility of a hotel. In general the days are not over-long, although there is some variation in the length and severity of each section.

Each Day opens with a summary table providing the distance to be walked, the altitude of various points on the walk, the amount of ascent and descent to be expected and the probable time that it would take the average walker to complete the stage. This is accompanied by a graphical profile of the standard route, so that the ascent and descent to be encountered can be easily appreciated. The summary table is followed in most cases by a reference section on optional excursions or alternative routes, so that the walker can see at a glance the various possibilities for the day. There follows a section on facilities so that the reader can plan ahead for the next day or two with regard to food, accommodation availability and other services. There are sub-sections on accommodation, shops, restaurants, cafés and bars and public transport. The text then begins with a short introductory passage describing the nature of the section and detailing the highlights of the stage. Quick reference to this introductory paragraph (under Summary) will reveal the character of each Day. Finally there is a full description of the route with special reference to any difficulties that may be encountered or any possible navigational problems. Most of the alternative routes and excursions are also described in detail here.

Distances and Altitudes
Distances and altitudes are given in miles and feet respectively, because most English-speaking people are familiar with this system, but also in kilometres and metres as this is how they appear on the maps. A very approximate but easily remembered conversion is: 1,000m is approximately 3,300ft; 2,000m is approximately 6,600ft; 3,000m is approximately 9,900ft.

There are difficulties in attempting to calculate distance covered on Alpine trails because of the numerous twists and turns on the route and the nature of the terrain traversed. For instance, climbing a hill by a series of tight zig-zags will obviously cover more ground than can be accurately measured on either a 1:50,000 or a 1:25,000 scale map. Newcomers to Alpine walking will soon come to realise that altitude gained and lost and the nature of the terrain itself are more reliable indicators of the severity of a stage than the mere distance to be covered.

Timings
For the above stated reasons, times as well as distances are given between the various stages. These times reflect what it is considered that the average rambler would maintain, but no allowance has been made for stopping to rest and/or admire the scenery, have lunch etc. This must be considered when estimating the time required for the

day's activities. The actual time taken will obviously vary from group to group and depend also on the prevalent conditions, although it is useful to have an indication of the time generally required to walk a section, (this is particularly true in the often steep and rugged terrain of the Alps). It is a system widely used in Europe: signposts en route will be encountered indicating the time required to walk to the next col, village, refuge or gîte d'étape.

Topographical Profiles
The height profiles, indicating the ascent and descent involved on each stage, are of the standard route of the Tour (including any excursions from the direct route that have been included in the main summary tables at the start of each Day). Note that the profiles do not include any of the suggested excursions not listed in the tables. Moreover profiles have not been given for the various alternative trails, however the information provided on them in the book should be sufficient to estimate the severity or otherwise of these routes.

Placenames
Occasionally there are alternative spellings for the names of cols, peaks and hamlets etc. This is particularly the case in the areas bordering Italy. In general the names and spellings used on the French maps have been adopted, but where there are alternatives then these have been given in the text.

SUMMARY TABLE

STAGE	DISTANCE		ASCENT		DESCENT		EST.TIME	
	miles	km	ft	m	ft	m	hrs	mins
1. DURANCE VALLEY TO FURFANDE	12.1	19.5	5997	1829	1429	436	8	00
2. FURFANDE TO CEILLAC	10.7	17.2	3494	1066	5369	1720	7	30
3. CEILLAC TO SAINT-VERAN	8.0	12.9	4225	1289	2976	908	5	45
4. SAINT-VERAN TO REFUGE AGNEL	8.1	13.0	3514	1072	1678	512	5	25
5. EXCURSION: LE PAIN DE SUCRE AND THE LAKES	8.8	14.2	3410	1040	3410	1040	6	20
6. REFUGE AGNEL TO REFUGE BAILLIF-VISO VIA THE SOUSTRA VALLEY (ITALY)	12.0	19.3	4135	1261	4528	1381	7	50
7. REFUGE BAILLIF-VISO TO LA MONTA VIA THE PELLICE VALLEY (ITALY)	8.1	13.0	3111	949	5730	1748	6	20
8. LA MONTA TO ABRIES	12.6	20.3	4646	1417	4901	1495	7	40
9. ABRIES TO LES FONDS DE CERVIERES	11.7	18.8	5203	1587	3721	1135	8	05
10. LES FONDS DE CERVIERES TO SOULIERS	6.7	10.8	2111	644	2738	835	4	30
11. SOULIERS TO BRUNISSARD	7.4	11.9	3606	1100	3927	1198	5	35
12. BRUNISSARD TO FURFANDE	6.5	10.5	3455	1054	1662	507	5	10
13. FURFANDE TO DURANCE VALLEY	12.2	19.6	731	223	5298	1616	5	50
TOTALS	124.9	201.0	47637	14531	47367	14531	84	00

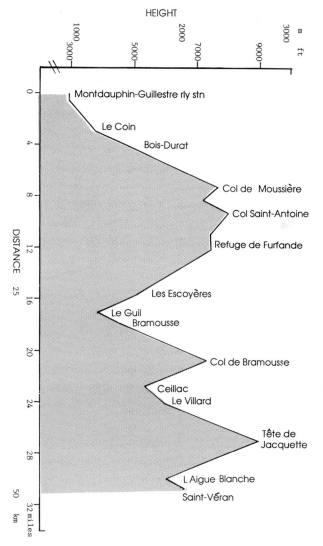

PROFILE OF DAYS 1-3

HEIGHT

HEIGHT

DISTANCE

Montdauphin-Guillestre rly stn

Le Coin

Bois-Durat

Col de Moussière

Col Saint-Antoine

Refuge de Furfande

Les Escoyères

Le Guil
Bramousse

Col de Bramousse

Ceillac
Le Villard

Tête de
Jacquette

L Aigue Blanche

Saint-Véran

GUIDE

DAY 1
Durance Valley to Furfande

DISTANCE: 12.1 miles (19.5km)
TOTAL ASCENT: 5,997ft (1,829m)
TOTAL DESCENT: 1,429ft (436m)

	Height Above Sea Level		Ascent/ Desc.		Est. Time	
					Sect.	Accum
	ft	m	ft	m	hr m	hr m
Gîte d'Etape d'Eygliers	2950	900				
Montdauphin-Guillestre Rly. Stn.	2950	900				
Le Coin	3829	1168	+879	+268	1.30	1.30
Cabane du Bois Durat	5055	1542	+1226	+374	1.10	2.40
Col du Moussière	7717	2354	+2662	+812	2.20	5.00
Lac du Lauzet	7229	2205	-488	-149	0.40	5.40
Col Saint-Antoine	8058	2458	-115	-35		
			+944	+288	1.05	6.45
Les Granges de Furfande	7474	2280	-826	-252		
			+243	+74	0.50	7.35
Refuge de Furfande	7517	2293	+43	+13	0.25	8.00

Note

Add 10 minutes to the timings if starting from the Gîte d'Etape d'Eygliers.

The distance above· has been calculated from Montdauphin-Guillestre railway station.

ALTERNATIVE START

	Height Above Sea Level		Ascent / Desc.		Est.. Time	
					Sect..	Accum
	ft	m	ft	m	hr m	hr m
Saint-Crépin	2967	905				
Cabane du Guillermin	4131	1260	+1164	+355	1.30	1.30
Le Coin	3829	1168	-498	-152		
			+197	+60	0.30	2.00

For those staying the night in Saint-Crépin there is an alternative route to Le Coin which is far superior to the road route from Montdauphin-Guillestre railway station. This is part of the GR 541 and is waymarked with the usual red and white paint stripes as it follows a pleasant track through woodland. This alternative start is described after the standard route.

ALTERNATIVE ROUTE

It is possible to reach the Refuge de Furfande on the GR 541 via Les Girards and Col Garnier. This is the reverse of the route used for the final descent to the Durance Valley (see Day 13). It is somewhat easier than the route described here and involves about 4,567ft (1,393m) of ascent. The walking time is approximately 7 hours 20 minutes.

FACILITIES
Accommodation

The Gîte d'Etape d'Eygliers is situated about 1/2 mile (0.8km) north-west of Montdauphin-Guillestre railway station, by the side of a small lake and near to a camping site. It is *not* in the village of Eygliers, which is 1 1/4 miles (2 km) to the east and 417ft (127m) above the Durance Valley. Note that the gîte can sometimes be block-booked by participants of the canoe/kayak courses held on the adjacent lake. There are possibilities for swimming, water sports and sunbathing here. It is a popular area during summer weekends.

There is plenty of alternative accommodation available in the vicinity. The Hôtel de la Gare is adjacent to the railway station and the Hôtel de la Durance is a few hundred yards further down the N 94 road (turn right from the station). There are many hotels as well as a youth hostel in Guillestre, which is only 5 minutes from the railway station by bus or taxi. Hotels can also be found in Montdauphin itself (the fortress town overlooking the valley) and in Saint-Crépin, a couple of miles to the north along the N 94. All of these towns are within walking distance of the railway station, although it may be more pleasant to take one of the taxis which can usually be found on the station forecourt.

There are several campsites in the neighbourhood; the nearest is adjacent to the gîte d'étape but there are others marked on the map to the south and west of Guillestre.

There is no accommodation after leaving the Durance Valley until the Refuge de Furfande at the end of the day. There are, however, a couple of wooden cabins which are normally left open and which could be used for shelter or even a bivouac in an emergency. The Refuge de Furfande has a resident guardian, but only from the beginning of July until the end of the first week in September. There is a winter room in the refuge which is left unlocked throughout the year. Note that wild camping is not allowed in Furfande.

Shops

The nearest grocery shop to Mondauphin-Guillestre railway station can be found by turning right on the main road (N 94) outside the station. A small shop is located about 150 yards along the road on the left. Guillestre is the largest town in the Queyras and has a good selection of supermarkets, grocers, bakers and delicatessens. Banks and several gift shops will also be found in Guillestre.

Grocery shops are also found in Montdauphin and in Saint-Crépin.

Restaurants, Cafés and Bars

Both the Hôtel de la Gare and the Hôtel de la Durance close to the railway station have restaurants which are open to non-residents. There are restaurants and cafés in both Montdauphin and Saint-Crépin, but the widest selection is to be found in Guillestre.

Granges Bernard, Soustra valley, Italy (Day 6).
Snow covered Pointe Joanne in centre background.

Snow covered peaks on the Franco-Italian border,
from Pointe Joanne (Day 6)

Monte Viso from the Refuge Baillif-Viso (Day 6/7)

Public Transport

There are buses from the forecourt of Montdauphin-Guillestre railway station to Guillestre, Vars les Claux, Ceillac, Château Queyras and Abriès.

Trains from Montdauphin-Guillestre travel to Briançon and to Gap and Valence.

(For full details of bus and train services see Appendix 2.)

SUMMARY

Whilst staying the the Durance Valley in the vicinity of the Gîte d'Etape d'Eygliers, take time to survey the hills to the east above the village of Eygliers and the hamlet of Le Coin. With the aid of a map the two routes up from the Durance Valley can be traced, i.e. the GR 541 and the GR 541 variant. The latter climbs to the left whilst the standard route ascends to the right to turn the corner and climb out of sight above the Gorges du Guil. The standard GR 541 is used on the descent (see Day 13) but the variant with its somewhat grander scenery is to be used on the long ascent to Furfande.

The climb to the Col de Moussière is a long and strenuous one and, perhaps, a rather testing introduction to mountain walking in the Alps. It will certainly separate the fit from the unfit and at the end of the day some may regret their lack of preparation for the holiday! However, once up in the mountains the rigours of the climb should be forgotten. On reaching the Col de Moussière the scenery changes abruptly from woodland and grassy hillsides to austere rocky ridges and rough scree slopes.

The Lac du Lauzet is a good spot for lunch before the short pull up to the second col of the day, Col Saint-Antoine. The descent from here leads to the verdant summer pastures of Furfande. Here at the Granges de Furfande there are a number of buildings, many of which are now used as holiday homes. The trail wanders amongst these to arrive at the first mountain hut of the Tour, the Refuge de Furfande. This is a magnificent spot below the Col de Furfande, with widespread views of the surrounding high mountains.

The first few miles of today's route to the hamlet of Le Coin is on roads. These are very minor and few vehicles will be encountered. However, as the day is a long one and at the start of the holiday (before the walker has become 'trail fit'), this part of the itinerary could be omitted by taking a taxi from the railway station up to Le Coin. This would also avoid the first 900ft (275m) of ascent.

ROUTE

Turn left at the railway station on the N'94 for a hundred yards or so and take the signposted D 37 climbing up to Eygliers. From the gîte d'étape take the small road heading across the camping area to cross the railway line at a level crossing, then continue to the main road. Cross the N 94 and carry on to join the D 37. Climb on this road, taking tracks wherever possible to cut off the numerous hairpins. Arrive in the village of Eygliers near to the church and take the minor road signposted to Le Coin.

On arriving at this hamlet search for a signpost indicating the GR 541 and the Col de Moussière (in 3 hours 30 minutes) and the Refuge de Furfande (in 6 hours). Climb on a path which later becomes a wide forest track, climbing gently towards the north to reach a wooden cabin, the Cabane du Bois Durat. This is normally left open and can be used for shelter and even an overnight stay, although there are no facilities whatsoever, only bare floorboards. Nevertheless the cabin is dry and secure.

Leave the track here and take the waymarked forest path, climbing steeply with a ravine over to the left. Cross several small streams and continue to climb, eventually emerging from the trees with fine views back down to the Durance Valley. The trail reaches grassy pastures and continues to climb on wide zig-zags on a good path (obvious even in mist). Yellow painted waymarks accompany the usual red / white GR waymarks. Pass a signpost indicating the way to the Col de Moussière and the Lac du Lauzet, then continue ever upwards until a final sharp pull leads you up to the Col de Moussière. Here is a signboard indicating the height of the col as 2,354m (7,717ft) whereas the map gives 2,352m (7,711ft).

The landscape is now one of rock and scattered pine trees. For those new to Alpine walking this is a good place to listen for the first sound of marmots. There are several colonies in this area between the two cols. Their friendly whistles will accompany the wayfarer for much of this Tour. The next objective, the Lac de Lauzet, can just be discerned from the Col de Moussière. Descend by a series of zig-zags on a stony path to reach the lake. This picturesque spot is an ideal place for a picnic and would also make a good site for an overnight camp. However, if contemplating the latter ensure that the tent is located well away from the scree from where there is a potential threat from stone falls.

Climb above the lake following waymarks (orange stripes now accompany the red/white ones) to the Col Saint-Antoine. Here is a wooden post, but the sign on it has long since gone. Descend (yellow waymarks have now reappeared) to reach the junction with the standard GR 541 at a grassy area marked on the map as 'Panneau'. There is a sign here indicating the way to the Refuge de Furfande. Note Col Garnier away to the south, this will be ascended on the last day of the Tour. Turn to the north to pass through an area where there are numerous chalets. Be sure not to take a path climbing up to the Col de Furfande, but instead follow the signposts eastwards on a fairly level path to reach the Refuge de Furfande (GTA). This mountain hut usually flies the EEC flag (blue with 12 yellow stars).

ALTERNATIVE START FROM SAINT-CREPIN

From near the church in Saint-Crépin take the D 738 road climbing towards the south-east. Just before the few scattered houses of Villaron-Haut, leave the road on a waymarked path off to the right, by a stone crucifix. It is important not to miss this junction (the road that climbs above the hamlet leads eventually to Le Villard). Follow a forest track with occasional views down to the Durance Valley.

Shelter can be obtained, if required, in the Cabane du Guillermin. This is not on the direct line of the route but can be found by first locating a small water source on the left of the track, then about 100 yards later, turning off to the left on an ascending track which leads in about 200 yards to the Cabane du Guillermin. This is normally left open and could provide an emergency bivouac for about six persons There is a small metal stove but neither tables nor chairs. Be sure to close the door on leaving. Return to the main track which remains more or less level all the way to the hamlet of Le Coin. Here the standard route to the Col de Moussière is joined (see above).

*   *   *

Furfande to Ceillac

DISTANCE: 10.7 miles (17.2 km)
TOTAL ASCENT: 3,494ft (1,066m)
TOTAL DESCENT: 5,639 ft (1,720m)

	Height Above Sea Level		Ascent / Des.		Est.. Time	
					Sect.. Accum	
	ft	m	ft	m	hr m	hr m
Refuge de Furfande	7517	2293				
Les Escoyères	5022	1532	-2495	-761	2.00	2.00
Bramousse	4590	1400	-1138	-347		
			+705	+215	1.45	3.45
Chalets de Bramousse	6032	1840	+1442	+440	1.15	5.00
Col de Bramousse	7379	2251	+1347	+411	1.10	6.10
Ceillac	5373	1639	-2006	-612	1.20	7.30

ALTERNATIVE ROUTES
(1) There is an alternative route from Les Escoyères to Ceillac via the hamlet of Montbardon (4,931ft/1,504m) where there is a gîte d'étape. From Montbardon the route climbs to Col Fromage (7,543ft/2,301m) from where the GR 5 is taken down to Ceillac. The route, which is also marked on the maps as the GR 58, involves approximately the same amount of ascent and descent as the standard, more direct route described here.
(2) There is another variant which may be taken from Bramousse to Ceillac. This route, which is marked on the maps, climbs to join the trail from Montbardon to Col Fromage. Once again the GR 5 is taken down to Ceillac.

Both of these alternative routes are worthwhile, but will be less appealing to those who have already followed the GR 5, or who intend to walk this trail at a later date.

FACILITIES
Accommodation
(1) A privately owned gîte is located in Bramousse.

(2) There is a gîte d'étape at Montbardon on the first alternative route (see above).

(3) Ceillac has a large gîte d'étape and several hotels.

Note that there is another gîte d'étape (Cime du Mélezet) 2 miles (3.2 km) south-east of Ceillac (off-route). There is also a campsite down the Mélezet Valley, just before Pied du Mélezet on the south side of the road, about $1^1/4$ miles (2 km) from Ceillac.

Shops
Limited food supplies may be available at a restaurant that is found by turning left on the D 902 below Les Escoyères (i.e. by making a short detour off-route). It may also be possible to obtain cheese, cooked meats, etc. at the farm in Bramousse. A far better selection will be found in Ceillac where there is a small supermarket and several other food shops. Ceillac has a post office (PTT) although this will not cash Eurocheques. There are also several gift shops in the village.

Restaurants, Cafés and Bars
These will be found in Ceillac. There is also a restaurant on the D 902 (see above).

Public Transport
There is a bus service from Ceillac to Montdauphin-Guillestre railway station (see Appendix 2).

SUMMARY
The Tour now joins the GR 58 heading south to Ceillac. Today's section is considerably easier than yesterday's route and starts with a long descent from Furfande, through the hamlet of Les Escoyères with its fine church, down to the D 902 road in the Combe de Queyras. The Col de Bramousse is the lowest col on the whole Tour and is

Les Escoyères

probably the easiest to ascend. The climb is always gradual and should present no problems. The other side of the pass is disfigured somewhat by the ski-lifts in the area, but the views south over to the Pic des Heuvières and the Italian border are particularly fine.

ROUTE
Descend on a clear path (the GR 58) to the south-east. In less than an hour a signpost is reached, indicating the GR 58 and Les Escoyères to the right and Le Queyron straight on. Take the path to the right, descending steeply to the left of a precipitous ravine. Ignore a further signpost indicating Le Queyron and continue on the path until a cross-track is met. Turn left and descend on the track through the hamlet of Les Escoyères. There is a water fountain here.

Remain on this track as it descends by a series of zig-zags to meet the road (D 902) in the valley bottom. Turn left for the restaurant and food supplies, but right to continue the Tour. After about $1/3$ mile (0.5 km) turn left to cross a footbridge over the river, then ascend on a

71

partly surfaced road to Bramousse where there is another water fountain. Many of the houses in this hamlet have been recently renovated. There are fine views back over the valley to Furfande.

Continue up the main track to climb through Bramousse, passing a house (Le Serre) and ignoring a path on the right which is signposted to a picnic spot. At a house called Le Pontet, a wooden bridge over a stream is reached. For the alternative route to Ceillac via Col Fromage, cross the bridge and follow the waymarked path. However, for the standard route of the GR 58 do not cross the bridge, but ascend on a path to the right instead. This path soon reaches a track which climbs by a series of zig-zags through shaded woodland, greatly appreciated on a hot, sunny day.

On seeing the Chalets de Bramousse ahead, leave the track and head straight for the buildings. Another water fountain will be found here. Climb up through the cluster of chalets and, where the buildings end, notice a signpost indicating a path to the Col de Souillet (45 minutes) and Col Fromage (2 hours). Ignore this and continue to climb on the main path through woodland. Nearing the top of the climb emerge from the trees, pass another sign indicating the Souillet and Fromage cols over to the left, and finally attain the Col de Bramousse. Here is a wide, open, grassy area, ideal for picnics. It is another good spot for observing marmots.

Descend first with the ski-lift on the left, but soon cross over the line of this and continue downhill with the ski-lift now on the right. On reaching the upper ski-station, pass in front of the building (do not go to the left of the station) heading west to find a path zig-zagging steeply down through woodland. Descend with a gorge over to the right to meet the road at the upper (new) end of the village of Ceillac. Wander down to the centre of the village, passing the new (1985) carpenter's cross and several gîtes and holiday homes. The gîte d'étape will be found close to the main shopping area (Centre Commercial).

The gîte d'étape (Les Baladins) is large but friendly. The rooms are small (generally for 6-8 people) each having a private shower and WC. Each room is named after a different Alpine flower. Dinner and

72

On the approach to Col Fromage

breakfast is available and a well equipped kitchen for self-caterers will be found in the basement.

*   *   *

Ceillac is the first of two places where the GR 58 and the GR 5 meet and cross (the other being Brunissard). From here the GR 5 heads south to leave the Queyras on its way into the département of the Alpes-de-Haute-Provence. Ceillac is situated on a level plain where two valley systems merge; the Melezet from the south and the Cristillan, a steep glacial hanging valley which runs east-west.

The village has expanded considerably during the last few years to accommodate the growing skiing trade. The skiing speciality of the Queyras is 'ski de Fond' which uses long, narrow skis and low shoes; Ceillac is the main centre for this sport. The skis used have a special lower surface that grips the snow and facilitates climbing. Ski de Fond is very popular in the area, is far less expensive than conventional downhill skiing and suitable for skiers of all ages.

Despite the expansion as a result of the skiing and tourist industries, and a plethora of holiday homes for sale and rent, Ceillac still retains its original character as a small farming community. There are many fine old buildings and the Church of Saint Sébastien, situated in the heart of the village, is of considerable architectural interest. (Music recitals are occasionally held in this church.) There is a second church in Ceillac; the Church of Sainte-Cécile has a conspicuous tall spire and is rather isolated from the village in an area known as La Clapière. There are two large carpenter's crosses in the town. These are a speciality of the region and are adorned with articles relating to the life and death of Christ (e.g. carpenter's tools, the Roman soldier's spear, the crown of thorns).

Ceillac is a very good centre for Alpine walking as there are no less than four high cols surrounding the village that can be attained on foot. Two are crossed on this Tour (the Col de Bramousse and the Col de Estronques) the other two (Col Fromage to the north and Col Giradin to the south) are both situated on the GR 5. It is interesting to try to locate the position of these cols from the High Street in Ceillac.

*   *   *

"Carpenter's Cross" at Ceillac

DAY 3

Ceillac to Saint-Véran

DISTANCE:	8.0 miles (12.9 km)
TOTAL ASCENT:	4,225ft (1,289m)
TOTAL DESCENT:	2,976ft (908m)

	Height Above Sea Level		Ascent/Desc.		Est.. Time Sect. Accum	
	ft	m	ft	m	hr m	hr m
Ceillac	5373	1639				
Le Villard	6032	1840	+659	+201	0.35	0.35
Col des Estronques	8691	2651	+2659	+811	2.15	2.50
Tête de Jacquette	9038	2757	+347	+106	0.20	3.10
Col des Estronques	8691	2651	-347	-106	0.15	3.25
Pont de Moulin	6062	1849	-2629	-802	1.50	5.15
Le Raux	6262	1910	+200	+61	0.10	5.25
Saint-Véran	6622	2020	+360	+110	0.20	5.45

OPTIONAL EXCURSIONS

(1) The ascent of the Tête de Jacquette (given below) is not essential, but highly recommended in good visibility as the view from the summit is superior to that from the col.

(2) Molines-en-Queyras and La Demoiselle Coiffée. The charming village of Molines-en-Queyras is about 3 miles (4.8 km) down the Aigue-Blanche Valley. It can be reached on foot, taxi or (possibly) bus down the D 5 road. If walking, remember that the return to Saint-Véran requires an ascent of about 1,000ft (305m). The famous La Demoiselle Coiffée (girl with a hat) is some $1^1/2$ miles (2.4 km) further down the valley in the Ravin de Prats below La Rua. Note that a taxi service operates from the gîte d'étape 'Les Gabelous', in Saint-Véran.

FACILITIES
Accommodation
Saint-Véran has two gîtes d'étape (Les Gabelous and Le Chant de l'Alpe), there are also several hotels in the village. Le Raux, just before and below Saint-Véran, has a small dortoir.
Shops
There are several grocery shops in Saint-Véran. The baker's shop is in the lower part of the village. There are also a number of gift shops in this small tourist and ski resort (local wood carvings are very popular).
Restaurants, Cafés and Bars
There are several in Saint-Véran.
Public Transport
There is an infrequent and seasonal bus service from Saint-Véran to Guillestre. Ask for details in the Queyras Regional Park Office near to the church in Saint-Véran. This office also has information on all aspects of the Queyras Park and will supply details of local events.

SUMMARY
Today's stage is quite short, a mere $7^1/2$ miles if excluding the ascent of the Tête de Jacquette. The latter is the first of several optional ascents of Alpine summits available on this Tour. It is a straightforward ascent to this peak and should present no problems. Although the distance involved is quite short, the climb to the Col des Estronques is fairly strenuous and unremitting.

There should be plenty of time available at the end of the day to explore the village of Saint-Véran, a good location for a rest day if required. There is a variety of accommodation on offer and an extra day would provide time to make an excursion down the Aigue-Blanche Valley to Molines-en-Queyras. A visit to the Demoiselle Coiffée is also recommended. This is quite a remarkable geological feature consisting of a tall pillar of earth topped by a large stone boulder. If time is not available to visit the latter, then the shape of this geological oddity can be seen on several of the postcards sold locally.

Looking south from the Col des Estronques

ROUTE

Locate the signpost near to the Church of Saint Sébastien in Ceillac, indicating the GR 58 to the Col des Estronques (3 hours 30 minutes) and to Saint-Véran (5 hours 30 minutes). Walk out of the village on the road heading north-east and pass a second carpenter's cross. Soon a GR sign is reached on the left-hand side of the road, indicating the GR 58 to the Col des Estronques and the GR 5 to Col Fromage. This path soon becomes a track which climbs to a few scattered chalets at an area known as Le Villard. It is here that the GR 5 leaves the GR 58, the former taking a path off to the left that heads for Col Fromage. The GR 58 continues on the track ahead. Just after passing an isolated chalet surrounded by trees on the left, be sure to take the signposted path off to the left. Soon a commemorative plaque to Philippe Lamour is reached. This man, a former mayor of Ceillac, was largely responsible for the development, waymarking and opening the of Tour du Queyras long-distance footpath. The well defined path continues by a series of seemingly endless zig-zags all the way to the

Col des Estronques. Allow plenty of time on this ascent to pause for catching one's breath and to admire the excellent views that unfold. The views towards the south and south-west of the mountains and the long serrated ridge above Lac Sainte-Anne are particularly fine.

The day should still be young and there will be ample time to take on the short excursion to the Tête du Jacquette, the peak to the east of the col. There is a path up to the summit, a climb of only some 350ft (106m). This ascent is recommended in fine weather as it opens out far wider views, particularly to the south-east and east, than are obtained from the col. From the summit a first sighting of Monte Viso (12,592ft/3,841m), Visolotto (10,976ft/3,348m) and Le Grand Queyras (10,209ft/3,114m) should be made. These giants of the region will be seen at closer quarters in a few days' time. The nearby Crête de Rasis is also seen to good advantage from the Tête de Jacquette, and the next objective, the village of Saint-Véran, is on view on the opposite side of the Aigue-Blanche Valley below.

If time is still available it may be possible to follow a path along the Crête de la Blavette to reach the Pointe des Marcelettes on the Sommet Jacquette. However, it is unlikely that there is an easy way down to the valley from here and so it would probably be necessary to retrace one's steps to the Tête de Jacquette.

Eventually a return must be made to the Col des Estronques. From here the descent to the Aigue-Blache Valley is on an obvious, well waymarked path. At the half-way mark on the descent, cross a stream and pass to the right of a green metal hut. Later pass through an area of woodland to reach and cross the Pont de Moulin over the River Aigue-Blance.

Ascend on a path to the hamlet of Le Raux from where you take the road climbing to Saint-Véran. Reach a T-junction at the lower end of the village and turn left for the gîte d'étape 'Le Chant de l'Alpe', right for the gîte d'étape 'Les Gabelous'.

* * *

Saint-Véran at 6,622ft (2,020m) has the distinction of being the highest continuously inhabited community in Europe. The village depends largely on tourism and particularly on the ski trade for its survival. Nevertheless it has resisted the more garish developments that mar so many French ski resorts and still retains the air of a simple mountain village. Much of the building is in wood and the houses are constructed in such a way as to avoid being in each other's shade. This makes full use of the warmth from the sun, so important at this altitude. The church is an interesting ornate building containing several gilded figures of the saints. Opposite the main entrance is another finely decorated carpenter's cross.

The Queyras is well known for its sundials (cadrans solaires) and several will be found in Saint-Véran, painted on the south-facing walls of a number of buildings. Perhaps the finest is that on the wall of the church. These painted sundials date back several centuries. Notice that the time indicated is nearly always an hour or more behind, perhaps because when these sundials were painted the local time was different from modern French summer time.

* * *

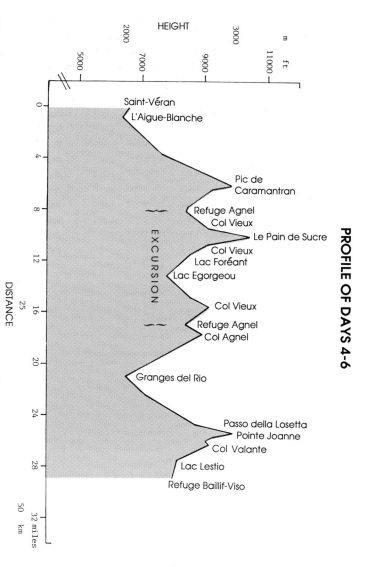

PROFILE OF DAYS 4-6

81

DAY 4

Saint-Véran to Refuge Agnel

DISTANCE   8.1 miles (13 km)
TOTAL ASCENT   3,514ft (1,072m)
TOTAL DESCENT   1,678ft (512m)

	Height Above Sea Level		Ascent/Desc		Est.. Time	
					Sect.	Accum
	ft	m	ft	m	hr m	hr m
Saint-Véran	6622	2020				
Road (Chapelle de Clausis)	7671	2340	-220	- 67		
			+1269	+387	1.40	1.40
Path junction	8166	2491	+495	+151	0.25	2.05
Col de Saint-Véran	9323	2844	+1157	+353	1.20	3.25
Pic de Caramantran	9917	3025	+593	+181	0.25	3.50
Col de Chamoussière	9323	2844	-593	-181	0.20	4.10
Refuge Agnel	8458	2580	-865	-264	1.15	5.25

ALTERNATIVE ROUTE

From the path junction there is a direct route to the Col de Chamoussière, omitting the Col de Saint-Véran and Pic de Caramantran. In fact the direct route is the true line of the GR 58, the path via the Col de Saint-Véran being a variant of the main route. However, if the weather is fine then the full route given above should be taken for the path presents no difficulties and the views of the mountains on the Franco-Italian border are first-rate. Moreover, the day is not a long one and there should be plenty of time to include the peak and the second col.

The direct route would save about 45 minutes and approximately

600ft (183m) of ascent and descent.

FACILITIES
Accommodation
Refuge Agnel is the only possibility en route for overnight accommodation (note that the Refuge de la Blanche is off-route). Agnel is a large, friendly and popular refuge which will provide dinner, breakfast and lunch on request. Unlike most CAF and CAI refuges, where there are no self-catering facilities, this GTA hut has stoves and a supply of utensils which may be used to prepare one's own food carried up from Saint-Véran.

Shops
Ensure that plenty of food is carried from Saint-Véran as no further grocery shops will be encountered for five days, and then only if the variation to Abriès is taken (see Day 8). However, in general it is only necessary to carry food for lunches. All of the gîtes d'étape and refuges en route will supply dinner and breakfast and in some of these establishments the food is of a very high quality and generous quantity.

Restaurants, Cafés and Bars
No such establishments will be passed en route. However, the Refuge Agnel will provide drinks of all types and snacks at most hours of the day.

Public Transport
There are no public transport facilities. The nearest taxi service from the Refuge Agnel is to be found in Molines-en-Queyras, 7^1/2 miles (12 km) down the valley from the refuge.

SUMMARY
For the first time on this Tour the walker will exceed 3,000m (9,835ft) above sea level, this is on the ascent to the Pic de Caramantran. The total amount of ascent on today's route is not excessive, however, as the journey starts in Saint-Véran at the 2,020m (6,622ft) mark. The route also has the distinction of reaching the two highest cols on any GR trail in France. The Col de Saint-Véran (2,844m/9,323ft) is actually

on a variant of the GR 58; so the distinction of the highest col on any GR route is usually awarded to the Col de Chamoussière. This is given as 2,844m (9,323ft) on IGN maps, but a board on the col itself registers a height of 2,842m (9,317ft) which would put it lower than the Col de Saint-Véran. However, this is all very academic (indeed the Col du Malrif on Day 9 is in fact higher than either of these!) and will be of little concern to the wayfarer, who is usually far more interested in the magnificent rock scenery in the region.

The day also holds another 'first'; the Franco-Italian border will be reached for the first time at the Col de Saint-Véran. Some caution is required on the descent from the Col de Chamoussière, particularly in wet weather when the path is very slippery. This section is probably the hardest on the standard route of the GR 58 being very steep and rocky, care should be exerted to prevent a stumble, although most walkers should find no real problems on this descent.

ROUTE

Leave the village of Saint-Véran on the road heading south-east. Soon leave this road on the right to descend to the river. Cross the bridge over the Aigue-Blanche and continue along a gently rising track with the river to the left. Pass a large ruined building over to the left and note the Chapelle de Clausis perched on the hillock ahead. Climb steeply to approach this and pass to the left of the chapel to meet the road. This road ends at the chapel and several parked cars will probably be found here, left by their owners who will be spending a day on the hills.

A notice-board here indicates the path to the Col de la Noire, Col Blanchet and the Refuge Blanche. Be sure to follow the red/white waymarks in the direction of the Col de Saint-Véran and the Col de Chamoussiere. Climb on this path until a second signboard is reached at a major path junction. Take the left fork to follow the red/white flashes of the GR 58 for the direct route to the Col de Chamoussière. However, for the Col de Saint-Véran continue straight on following yellow waymarks which accompany the usual red/white flashes. There are excellent views ahead of the mountains forming the

At the Col de Saint-Véran (pointed peak is the Tête des Toillies)

frontier with Italy. Particularly fine is the pointed spire of the Tête des Toillies. Do not be misled into thinking that the board seen ahead on the horizon is at the Col de Saint-Véran. On arrival it will be found to be another notice-board indicating a path to the Col de Chamoussière to the left and another to the Col de la Noire to the right; the route to the Col de Saint-Véran still lies straight ahead. At long last the col in question and the border with Italy will be reached.

At the Col de Saint-Véran there are fine views of the rocky ridge forming the Franco-Italian border. A prominent path descends into Italy and another passes along the ridge heading towards the impressive Rocca Bianca (10,028ft/3,059m). Our path, however, turns to the left (north-north-east) to climb the Pic de Caramantran. The 593ft (181m) of ascent to the summit may seem particularly strenuous; this may well be psychological as one climbs above the magical 3,000m (9,835ft) mark for the first time. There are occasional yellow marks on rocks to guide the ascent, but in any case the path is fairly obvious. The very top is all rock.

Descend carefully to the north for a 100 yards or so and then follow the ridge downhill to the left to reach the signboard at the Col de Chamoussière. Here the GR 58 is re-joined for a descent to the Refuge Agnel. The line of the descent is never in doubt, but some care is required as it descends steeply over schist and scree. The rocks can be very slippery and the path is often wet. In rain great care would be required to prevent a slip, which would be most painful on the sharp, hard rocks. In high winds there would also be a danger from stone falls from the scree above. The Refuge Agnel can in fact be seen from the col, but it will take well over an hour to reach it. The refuge is situated high up in the Agnel Valley, just below the Col Agnel.

On the descent from the Col de Chamoussière, the impressive peaks of the Pain de Sucre and Pic d'Asti should be on view. Le Pain de Sucre, which is the objective for tomorrow's excursion, bears little resemblance to the Sugarloaf in South Wales, known to many British hillwalkers.

DAY 5

Excursion: Le Pain de Sucre, Lac Foréant
and Lac Egourgéou

DISTANCE   8.8 miles (14.2 km)
TOTAL ASCENT   3,410ft (1,040m)
TOTAL DESCENT   3,410ft (1,040m)

| | Height Above Sea Level | | Ascent/Desc. | | Est. Time | |
| | | | | | Sect. | Accum |
	ft	m	ft	m	hr m	hr m
Refuge Agnel	8458	2580				
Col Vieux	9199	2806	+741	+226	0.40	0.40
Le Pain de Sucre	10517	3208	+1318	+402	1.10	1.50
Col Vieux	9199	2806	-1318	-402	0.50	2.40
Lac Foréant	8583	2618	-616	-188	0.20	3.00
Lac Egourgéou	7848	2394	-735	-224	1.00	4.00
Lac Foréant	8583	2618	+735	+224	1.15	5.15
Col Vieux	9199	2806	+616	+188	0.35	5.50
Refuge Agnel	8458	2580	-741	-226	0.30	6.20

ALTERNATIVES

(1) It would of course, be quite feasible to omit either the ascent of the mountain or the excursion to the lakes. Col Vieux is the key to the day's activities.

(2) The standard route of the GR 58 takes the path from Col Vieux down past the two lakes to reach the River Guil, Guil Valley and the gîte d'étape at La Monta (see Day 7). This trail from Refuge Agnel to La Monta takes about 4 hours. It is a splendid walk but lacks the grandeur of the Italian section (see Days 6 and 7). Nevertheless, for those with less time available, it would provide a most convenient route to La Monta. The route is described at the end of this section.

FACILITIES
A second night is to be spent at the Refuge Agnel. The notes on facilities given for Day 4 apply equally to Day 5. Refuge Agnel is the only source of food and shelter.

SUMMARY
After four days of carrying a pack over steep mountain passes, it is a good idea to give the shoulders and back a rest and have a day off in the high mountains. Refuge Agnel is a good place for such a day as it is situated at a high altitude and there are a variety of walking excursions available in the area. Moreover, if not too crowded, the refuge is a pleasant place to stay a while.

There are several possibilities for today. Having a complete rest day in the vicinity of the hut would be pleasant enough. For the more energetic and adventurous an ascent of Le Pain de Sucre (10,517ft/ 3,208m) can be made. This is the highest point reached on the walk and the first time that an altitude of 10,000ft will be exceeded. The peak appears to be quite formidable, but under good conditions the average hillwalker should experience few problems, provided the waymarked route is followed to the top. It is a fairly easy, albeit steep scramble to the summit. The peak should not, however, be tackled in adverse conditions, especially in rain, snow, high winds or when the mountain in enveloped in mist. The mountain should be left alone when covered in ice and snow, except by those with the correct equipment and experience. The guardian of the hut will offer advice on local weather conditions.

The second recommended excursion from the Refuge Agnel, for those not wishing to climb a high mountain, is a trip to the two lakes north of Col Vieux (Lac Foréant and Lac Egourgéou). In this upper valley there are several suitable places for a picnic, with good views back to Le Pain de Sucre and Pic d'Asti.

Neither the ascent of Le Pain de Sucre nor the walk to the lakes will take more than a few hours and so it is recommended that both trips are taken. If the mountain is climbed in the morning, then the afternoon could be spent over a lakeside picnic before returning over

Col Vieux to Refuge Agnel for dinner.

ROUTE

To reach Col Vieux leave Refuge Agnel and cross the road. Follow a good footpath which soon turns to climb towards the north-east. Pass a grassy plateau and a sign indicating that camping is permissible for one night only. Continue upwards to reach the col. On this climb Le Pain de Sucre will be clearly visible and the walker may become convinced that an ascent is out of the question. The mountain is deceptive; it is not so difficult as it may at first appear!

On reaching the col turn right to climb the shoulder of the mountain on a good path. The angle of the main peak begins to look less severe, although the mountain still presents a considerable obstacle. The path levels for a short while before the scramble to the summit begins. At the start of the climb it is easy to go astray so do not go on until the waymarks are found and followed. The easiest line is waymarked with small cream-coloured arrows and crosses (either means that the route is correct). The correct way heads over towards the right at the start of the climb. Only those with experience should attempt an ascent by any other route, of which there are several possibilities. If in doubt, always retreat. The route is also marked in places by small stone cairns.

The narrow summit is marked by a metal cross. Here there is also a metal tube containing a book for those who have reached the summit to record their names. The close-up view of the sheer rock faces of the adjacent Pic d'Asti is awe inspiring. The panorama is extensive. The large mass of mountain to the north-west is the Grand Queyras (10,209ft/3,114m). Le Pain de Sucre really is a lofty perch, the sort of position normally the preserve of the dedicated Alpinist. Retreat carefully, reversing the line of ascent to reach the path on the shoulder of the mountain. Follow this back to Col Vieux.

Descend to the north on the GR 58 signposed 'Les Lacs'. The first lake, Lac Foréant, is soon reached. The spot is most picturesque and a favourite haunt of anglers. Lac Foréant provides a good place for lunch after the thrills of the morning on Le Pain de Sucre. Descend

The sheer rock face of Pic d'Asti from the summit of Le Pain de Sucre

further on the path until Lac Egourgéou comes into view. The relatively flat area just before this lake is usually teeming with marmots and so is a good place for observing these charming animals if they haven't yet been encountered (which is most unlikely!). It is pointless going beyond Lac Egourgéou as the route must now be reversed and the way made back over Col Vieux for a second night at the refuge.

DIRECT ROUTE FROM REFUGE AGNEL TO LA MONTA

Take the route over Col Vieux to Lac Foréant and on to Lac Egourgéou as described above. Continue on this obvious path, waymarked throughout with red/white flashes. Descend through woodland arriving eventually in the Guil Valley at a small wooden shelter close to a bridge across the River Guil. The shelter has a table and a raised wooden sleeping area accommodating about four people. Do not cross this bridge, but instead continue to a second bridge which is about 3/4 mile (1.2 km) further on. For Ristolas (hotel, restaurant and new gîte d'étape) continue ahead (approx. 30 minutes); but for La Monta, cross the bridge and head for the church and gîte d'étape across the road.

DAY 6

Refuge Agnel to Refuge Baillif-Viso
via the Soustra Valley (Italy)

DISTANCE	12 miles (19.3 km)
TOTAL ASCENT	4,135ft (1,261m)
TOTAL DESCENT	4,528ft (1,381m)

	Height Above Sea Level		Ascent/Desc.		Est. Time Sect. Accum	
	ft	m	ft	m	hr m	hr m
Refuge Agnel	8458	2580				
Col Agnel	8996	2744	+538	+164	0.40	0.40
Granges del Rio	6557	2000	-2439	-744	1.40	2.20
Granges Bernard	7147	2180	+590	+180	0.25	2.45
Passo della Losetta	9409	2870	+2262	+690	2.10	4.55
Pointe Joanne	10005	3052	+597	+182	0.30	5.25
Passo della Losetta	9409	2870	-597	-182	0.20	5.45
Col de Valante	9228	2815	-279	-90		
			+115	+35	0.40	6.25
Lac Lestio	8228	2510	-1000	-305	0.55	7.20
Refuge Baillif-Viso	8065	2460	-197	- 60		
			+33	+10	0.30	7.50

OPTIONAL EXCURSION

The ascent of Pointe Joanne can be omitted if time is short or the conditions unfavourable. However, the peak is a sensational vantage point from which to view Monte Viso and the jagged, rocky mountains of the Franco-Italian border; an ascent is therefore highly recommended. A return must be made from Pointe Joanne to the Passo della Losetta before continuing the itinerary.

FACILITIES

Accommodation

There is a gîte d'étape in Chianale in Italy (off-route). Otherwise the only accommodation available is the CAF Refuge Baillif-Viso. The refuge provides dinner and breakfast (and possibly lunch). Self-caterers must bring their own stove, fuel and utensils. A reduction in overnight fee (usually 50%) will be given to members of a recognised Alpine club or to holders of a Reciprocal Rights Card. There is a shower, but it provides only cold water.

Shops

Food may be bought in the village of Chianale in Italy, but this will require a considerable detour from the route. French francs will probably be accepted here (but beware of the exchange rate).

Restaurants, Cafés and Bars

The only such establishments in the area are those that may be found in Chianale. The Refuge Baillif-Viso will provide drinks and snacks if required.

Public Transport

There is none available.

SUMMARY

This stage is the first of two excursions into Italy. The border is soon reached at Col Agnel, which is thought by scholars to be one of the possible crossing places used by Hannibal and his elephants on their journey over the Alps into Italy. After a long descent to the south down the Vallone dell Agnello, the route changes direction to climb, gradually at first, up the isolated Soustra Valley. After a stiff climb to an Italian ridge at the Passo della Losetta, there is an optional ascent of Point Joanne.

The highlight of this part of the journey is the close-up view of the north-west face of Monte Viso, almost 1,000m (3,278ft) of very steep rock. This really is a most impressive mountain that deserves to be better known outside the region. It ranks amongst the most spectacular of the Alpine peaks. The mountain stands alone, wholly in Italy, and at 12,592ft (3,841m) it towers above all the other peaks in the vicinity.

The Soustra Valley, Italy

Monte Viso is seen to best advantage from the balcony path between the Passo della Losetta and Col de Valante. France is re-entered at this col and a night is spent at the Refuge Baillif-Viso. The latter stages of the route from just below the Passo della Losetta to the refuge are co-incident with the Italian Monviso Tour (see p.16).

It is interesting how the culture changes abruptly from one country to the next, even in these high Alpine valleys. The mountains are a very effective barrier. Once over the col and into Italy, suddenly everything and everybody appears to be Italian. Remember to change your usual greeting from 'Bonjour' to 'Buon Giorno'!

ROUTE
On leaving the Refuge Agnel walk back on the path towards the Col de Chamoussière, but after about 500 yards leave this to head south-east towards Col Agnel, following red/white waymarks. A dirt road also leads to the col. This was being resurveyed during September 1988 and it is likely that it will be surfaced in the future.

The border between France and Italy is reached at the Col Agnel, where there is a customs post although customs officers seldom appear to be on duty there. The road on the Italian side is surfaced. Paths leading down the valley cross this road on several occasions but are neither well waymarked nor easy to follow. If both route and patience are lost then the easy answer is to follow the road downhill (there is relatively little traffic and the road is quite a feat of engineering).

The road descends to the south for a considerable distance before negotiating a huge U-turn to swing round towards the north. From this point on there is a good view down to the village of Chianale. If time is available then a visit to this charming community is recommended. The village is protected from modern development by the Italian Government and so the houses and way of life are much as they were centuries ago. Simply continue on the road to reach the village.

If not visiting Chianale, descend on the road as far as the Granges del Rio. Just before the buildings take the footpath on the left signposted to the Soustra Valley and the Passo della Losetta. This path is waymarked with red/white flashes and also with an orange-red stripe. Follow the path to the north-east, gradually climbing up this most beautiful valley. A wide Alpine pasture is reached at the Granges Bernard. The path becomes a little indistinct at this point; walk between the scattered buildings keeping the river over to the right. The objectives of today's climb can be seen clearly ahead - the Passo della Losetta and the peak named Pointe Joanne to its left. Be sure to turn round several times on the ascent to admire this most photogenic valley.

After crossing the river the climb begins in earnest. It is well waymarked with red/white and orange-red stripes. Climb steeply to pass a small stone building used for animals, then zig-zag on the scree and schist slopes on the final approach to the pass. Care would be required here in wet conditions. One final long pull across the scree and schist leads to the Passo della Losetta whose name is painted in large letters on a prominent boulder at the top.

The summit of Pointe Joane

If the hour is late or the weather uncertain, the route should be followed to Col Valante. In good conditions an excursion to the summit of Pointe Joanne is recommended. This detour should certainly not be taken in mist since to lose the correct line of ascent and descent on this peak would probably have disastrous consequences. However, in clear, calm weather no problems should be encountered.

For Pointe Joanne take the path climbing the ridge to the north of the pass. About 30 minutes effort will lead to the cross on the summit of the mountain, which just exceeds an altitude of 10,000ft. There are

Mt Aiguillette from the Col de Sellière (Day 7

The church at La Monta (Day 7/8)

precipitous drops on nearly every side. The view of the surrounding rock peaks is quite outstanding. The dominating feature is the north-west face of Monte Viso. This mountain was a favourite with British climbers in the last century, so much so that one of its glaciers is named after Coolidge, the famous mountaineer. The attendant Visolotto, Pointe Castaldi and Pointe de Rome also hold the attention. The border runs to the west along the Crête de Motte to Mont Aiguillette and Pic d'Asti. The view south to the Punta Tre Chiosis is also admirable. The Matterhorn and Monte Rosa may be discerned in the far distance. A much better view is obtained from Pointe Joanne than from Passo della Losetta, so even non-peakbaggers should consider the extra 600ft (183m) of ascent to be effort well spent!

Return by the same route to the Passo della Losetta and continue on the red/white waymarked path zig-zagging downhill. Soon after passing a large ruined building the path divides. The path descending straight ahead leads to the Rifugio Gagliardone (CAI) and on to the larger Rifugio Vallanta (CAI). To continue the Tour be sure to take the path to the left. This contours around the scree and schist slopes of Pointe Joanne. Whilst traversing on this balcony path there are close-up views of Monte Viso's mighty north-west face.

The border between France and Italy is reached again at Col de Valante (Passo di Vallanta). Descend into France down a narrow rock gully, followed by a seemingly endless scree slope. There are plenty of rocks and boulders to negotiate which may become very slippery in wet weather. Follow the red/white waymarks carefully to descend 1,000ft (305m) to Lac Lestio. From the lake there is a good path leading to the Refuge Baillif-Viso.

The Refuge Baillif-Viso belongs to CAF. The first refuge on this site was opened in 1902 and there is an interesting photograph on the wall of the dining room showing climbers and celebrities at the opening ceremony. A new hut, built in 1976, has replaced this original refuge. The hut has provided accommodation over the years for the many people walking up the valley to view Monte Viso. The road now ends at the Belvédère du Viso, only just over 1,000ft (305m) below and about $1^1/4$ miles (2 km) from the refuge (so the hut has

The Vallanta Valley

many day visitors). The refuge is in a superb location in the upper
Guil Valley. From the balcony there is a first rate view of Monte Viso
which is perfectly framed at this point by the steep ridges rising from
Col Valante. With the aid of a pair of binoculars it is possible to pick
out the cross on the summit of Pointe Joanne. Watch for the setting
sun on the summit crags of Monte Viso, which is particularly
impressive if the upper slopes of the mountain are covered in snow.
This is a magnificent sight for any lover of the high mountains.

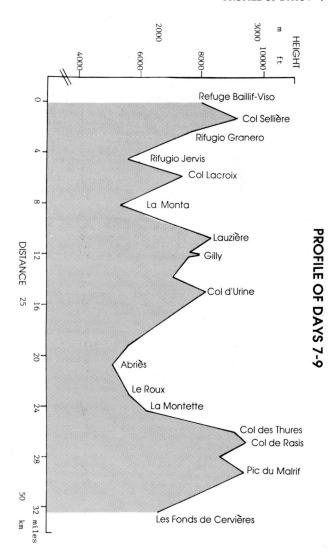

PROFILE OF DAYS 7-9

HEIGHT

m

ft

2000

3000

4000

6000

8000

10000

DISTANCE

0

4

8

12

25

16

20

24

28

50

32

km

miles

Refuge Baillif-Viso
Col Sellière
Rifugio Granero
Rifugio Jervis
Col Lacroix
La Monta
Lauzière
Gilly
Col d'Urine
Abriès
Le Roux
La Montette
Col des Thures
Col de Rasis
Pic du Malrif
Les Fonds de Cervières

DAY 7

Refuge Baillif-Viso to La Monta
via the Pellice Valley (Italy)

DISTANCE	8.1 miles (13.0 km)
TOTAL ASCENT	3,111ft (949m)
TOTAL DESCENT	5,730ft (1,748m)

	Height Above Sea Level		Ascent/Desc.		Est. Time	
					Sect.	Accum
	ft	m	ft	m	hr m	hr m
Refuge Baillif-Viso	8065	2460				
Col Sellière	9291	2834	+1226	+374	1.10	1.10
Rifugio Granero	7792	2377	-1524	-465		
			+26	+8	0.55	2.05
Rifugio Jervis	5678	1732	-2114	-645	1.40	3.45
Col Lacroix	7537	2299	+1859	+567	1.20	5.05
La Monta	5445	1661	-2092	-638	1.15	6.20

OPTIONAL EXCURSIONS AND ALTERNATIVE ROUTES
Ascent of Monte Granero

	Height Above Sea Level		Ascent/Desc.		Est. Time	
					Sect.	Accum.
	ft	m	ft	m	hr m	hr m
Rifugio Granero	7792	2377				
Monte Granero	10379	3166	+2587	+789	2.30	2.30
Rifugio Granero	7792	2377	-2587	-789	1.30	4.00

Most walkers will find the day quite iong enough without the ascent and descent of a major peak. However, Monte (or Punta) Granero is a fine mountain and a climb to the summit can be made on a waymarked route from the Rifugio Granero. The climb involves 2,587ft of ascent and takes about 2 hours 30 minutes from the refuge. Hence those wishing to include the mountain on their itinerary would probably have to stay the night at Rifugio Granero or Rifugio Jervis. It would then be possible to get back on schedule by taking a variant route from the Rifugio Jervis to the Col d'Urine (marked on the IGN maps as GR 58B), omitting La Monta and walking from the Pellice Valley to Abriès or Le Roux in one day (approx. 5 hours from Rifugio Jervis to Abriès).

The ascent of Monte Granero requires some scrambling ability and should not be attempted by the inexperienced. It should certainly be avoided in mist or bad weather. The guardian of Rifugio Granero should be able to supply information on the weather and conditions on the mountain.

Col de la Traversette (Collè delle Traversette)

Another interesting excursion from the Refuge Baillif-Viso is the climb to the Col de la Traversette (9,661ft/2,497m), south of the Aiguille de la Traversette on the Franco-Italian border. The col is well worth a visit as nearby there is a fascinating short tunnel (Buco di Viso) through the mountain, allowing passage to the other side of the ridge. This is thought to be the first tunnel ever to be constructed in the Alps. It was built in the 18th century to allow merchants to transport salt and other commodities for trade in the valleys to the east, now part of Italy. (Many centuries ago the border was in fact much further to the east and Monte Viso was at one time on French soil.)

There is a steep descent from the Col de la Traversette down into Italy to the Pian del Re where the source of the River Po, the longest river in Italy, is. There is also an albergo (a mountain hotel) at Pian del Re. This trail forms part of the Italian Monviso Tour.

Direct Route to La Monta

For those short of time, it is possible to take a path from Refuge Baillif-Viso to descend to the road head at the Belvédère du Viso, then on the road from there to La Monta. The route remains in France throughout. It is not recommended except in bad weather or as a quick route back to civilisation.

L'Echalp

A stroll along the river and a visit to the picturesque hamlet of L'Echalp is a relaxing way to work off an evening meal at La Monta. The route is described at the end of this stage.

FACILITIES

Accommodation

There are several possibilities for overnight accommodation on this stage. The gîte d'étape at La Monta and the Italian refuges of Granero and Jervis are spaced well apart. As well as Rifugio Jervis there is also a pension in the hamlet of Ciabot del Pra. Another gîte d'étape and a hotel are to be found at Ristolas further down the Guil Valley from La Monta.

Shops

There are neither shops on the main route nor on any of the alternative trails or excursions. Food may possibly be bought at the village of Ristolas, about 30 minutes walk down the valley from La Monta.

Restaurants, Cafés and Bars

As for shops (see above). The refuges and gîtes d'étape all supply meals, snacks and drinks. The restaurant at the gîte d'étape in La Monta (on the first floor) is open to non-residents. The food is excellent and the helpings are large. There is also a restaurant at Ristolas.

Public Transport

There are no public transport facilities.

SUMMARY

Today's route involves the second and final excursion into Italy. The scenery is once again of the highest order, with the giant Monte Viso still dominating the scene for much of the day. The upper Guil Valley is an odd, trapped little corner of France, surrounded on three sides by Italy.

From the Refuge Baillif-Viso the trail climbs to re-enter Italy at Col Sellière. A steep descent leads to the tranquil Lago Lungo and the Rifugio Granero, from where there is the optional ascent of Monte Granero for experienced hillwalkers. The Pellice Valley is descended until Ciabot del Pra where there is a second Italian refuge. A return to France is then made via Col Lacroix and the evening is spent in the tiny hamlet of La Monta, which consists only of a gîte d'étape and a church.

ROUTE

From the Refuge Baillif-Viso follow the red/white waymarks heading north over a flat area. After crossing a river, the climb to the border commences and soon a rather old sign is passed indicating the way to the Col de la Traversette. About 100 yards further on, the Monviso Tour is left where a GR 58 variant sign indicates the route to La Monta via Col Sellière. The trail climbs towards the north and is perhaps longer and steeper than it at first appears. The route is fairly obvious and heads for the lowest point on the rocky skyline. If this ascent is tackled early in the morning then it should be achieved all in shade. At the col there are good views of Monte Viso and Mont Aiguillette. Descend into Italy, steeply at first over schist (take care) but on an obvious red/white waymarked path. The path descends to a small lake (Lago Lungo) in a superb mountain setting. Cross the stepping stones and climb a little above the lake to turn right on a path (signposted Rifugio 100m) leading to the Granero refuge.

The superb view down the Pellice Valley can be enjoyed from the tables outside the entrance to the refuge. The impressive Monte Granero is seen to perfection from here. Those wishing to make the ascent are advised to book their places in the refuge before leaving for the summit (it might be full on your return). To begin the climb follow the yellow arrows from the hut.

For the standard route return to the path descending into the Pellice Valley. After a while the path divides; follow the yellow arrows to the right (the alternative path to the left also descends the valley to Partia d'Amunt, but on the opposite side of the stream). Drop steeply to cross a stream and follow the arrows down through sparse woodland to reach a grassy track on flatter ground. Follow this to cross an earthen/log bridge across the river to enter the hamlet of Partia d'Amunt. Here in this high Italian Alpine valley, a simple rustic existence has continued unchanged for many centuries. Follow the track passing through the hamlet and continue ahead on this over level ground towards the hamlet of Ciabot del Pra.

Pass the small cluster of houses at Ciabot del Pra and, about 150 yards before Rifugio Jervis, seek a path over to the left. This starts just to the left of the small chasm and stream (note the house built into the rock to the right of this). On arriving at the foot of the climb a GTA sign and red/white waymarks should be found. Climb on a well made path zig-zagging up the mountainside. The trees may provide welcome shade from the sun as the tinkling of cow bells in the lower pasture and the voices of Italian holidaymakers float up the hillside from below. The path would be exceedingly steep if it were not for the many expertly made zig-zags. The col has a false summit where one arrives at a balcony path. Here there are excellent views back up the Pellice Valley ending in the shapely peak of Monte Granero with the grand Monte Viso again on display. The balcony path climbs fairly easily to Col Lacroix (Col de la Croix) where there is indeed an old cross and also a small stone hut. Peer inside the latter to find a quote from Lord Baden-Powel of Gillwell, painted on the wall in Italian. Food for thought.

Leave Italy behind and descend once more into France on a clear path, soon passing a yellow sign indicating the way to La Monta. Note that there is another path which crosses the stream on the left and continues downhill, eventually emerging by the side of the church in the village of L'Echalp. However, for La Monta remain on the main path soon passing the ruins of an old refuge (Refuge Napoléon). Continue the descent to enter woodland. The path drops steeply through the trees and use should be made of any available zig-zags to avoid undue strain on the knees. After a while the valley and road will be seen below. On reaching the road turn right and, in about 100 yards, pass the sign indicating La Monta. This is a charming little hamlet which consists of a church with an attractive bell tower, a cemetery and a fine gîte d'étape. The guardian's husband speaks perfect English - a great relief to those walkers with little French!

L'Echalp

If time and energy are still available then a stroll along the river to the hamlet of L'Echalp passes a pleasant hour. Cross the road in front of the gîte d'étape at La Monta and bear to the left to find a bridge across the River Guil. Cross the bridge and turn to the left (turning right leads in about 30 minutes to the larger village of Ristolas). Follow the red/white GR 58 waymarks up the valley until a second bridge is reached by a small wooden cabin. Here cross back over the river and pass through a car parking area. Turn left on the road for a few yards to take the small road up to L'Echalp, where there is a telephone.

L'Echalp is much larger than La Monta, having several ancient stone houses with old wooden verandahs. It is a centre for artists and for the production and sale of Queyras honey. A return to La Monta may be made back along the river, or alternatively, if the traffic is not too heavy, the road leads back to the gîte d'étape in 10 minutes. (A touching memorial is passed alongside this road; the plaque states that during the Second World War five men from this tiny community were killed in action.)

DAY 8

La Monta to Le Roux or Abriès

DISTANCE	To Le Roux 11.1 miles (17.9 km)
	To Abriès 12.6 miles (20.3 km)
TOTAL ASCENT	4,646ft (1,417m)
TOTAL DESCENT	To Le Roux 4,353ft (1,328m)
	To Abriès 4,901ft (1,495m)

	Height Above Sea Level		Ascent/Desc.		Est. Time	
					Sect.	Accum
	ft	m	ft	m	hr m	hr m
La Monta	5445	1661				
Sommet de la Lauzière	8445	2576	+3000	+915	2.30	2.30
Collette de Gilly	7720	2355	-724	-221	0.40	3.10
Sommet de Gilly	8088	2467	+367	+112	0.15	3.25
Collette de Gilly	7720	2355	-367	-112	0.10	3.35
Col d'Urine	8278	2525	-525	-160		
			+1082	+330	1.45	5.20
Le Roux	5737	1750	-2737	-835		
			+197	+60	1.55	7.15
(Abriès)	5190	1583	-3285	-1002		
			(+197	+60)	(2.20)	(7.40)

OPTIONAL EXCURSIONS

Ascent of the Tête du Pelvas

	Height Above Sea Level		Ascent/Desc.		Est. Time	
					Sect.	Accum
	ft	m	ft	m	hr m	hr m
Col d'Urine	8278	2525				
Tête du Pelvas	9602	2929	+1324	+404	1.45	1.45
Col d'Urine	8278	2525	-1324	-404	1.15	3.00

From the Col d'Urine on the Franco-Italian border the peakbagger has a choice of two summits, La Mait d'Amunt (9,192ft/2,804m) to the north-east or the much more impressive Tête du Pelvas (Mon Palavas) at 9,602ft (2,929m) to the south-west of the col. The latter peak is quite a notable landmark in the area and a superb panorama of the Italian Alps is to be had from its summit. However, its ascent involves a steep scramble over loose rocks and scree and should not be attempted by the inexperienced. In good conditions this peak is recommended to the practised hillwalker; it is a minor classic. The ascent of the Tête du Pelvas is described at the end of the section. (Note that the ascent of this peak, combined with the route described, makes for a very long day.)

ALTERNATIVE ROUTES

There are several ways to vary and shorten today's itinerary. The main possibilities are:

(1) Follow the GR 58 down the Guil Valley from La Monta to Ristolas and ascend, still on the GR 58, to the Collette de Gilly. From here the GR 58 can be followed to the north-east to join the route descending to Le Roux or Abriès. (Approx. time of 6 hours 15 minutes, 2,500ft (763m) of ascent.)

(2) From La Monta to Collette de Gilly via the Sommet de la Lauzière as described, but then omitting the detour to the Col d'Urine. The GR 58 can be followed instead directly from the Collette de Gilly to Le Roux or Abriès, as in (1) above. (Approx. time of 6 hours 40 minutes, 3,000ft (915m) of ascent.)

(3) The shortest and easiest route to Abriès from La Monta is to follow the GR 58 to Ristolas (much damaged in the Second World War but now rebuilt) and then take the road further down the valley to Abriès. (Approx. time of 1 hour 20 minutes, no ascent.) The route is not recommended except in bad weather or to save time if the holiday has to be cut short.

This stage has two alternative finishing points, Le Roux or Abriès. The choice of finishing place will depend mainly upon two factors; the route planned for the climb to the Col and Pic du Malrif on the following day, and whether the walker needs to re-provision with food.

Both Le Roux and Abriès have gîtes d'étape but the former is only a hamlet with no shops. However Le Roux is the ideal starting point for the recommended walk to the Col du Malrif via the Col des Thures and the Col de Rasis (see Day 9). Abriès is much larger with several grocery shops and small supermarkets. Purchasing food may be a high priority at this stage since the last shop was encountered at Saint-Véran, some five days ago. There is a direct route from Abriès to the Col du Malrif via the Lac du Grand Laus (see Day 9, Alternative Route) which is scenically of high quality and without the navigational difficulties that some may experience on the route via the Col des Thures. Therefore some walkers may prefer to finish today at Abriès, stock up with supplies and take the direct route to the Col du Malrif where the route from the Col des Thures is joined.

Alternatively, if it is necessary to buy food in Abriès, then the route to the Col des Thures can still be taken by first walking to Le Roux. The hamlet can be reached by a walk of about $2^1/4$ miles (3.6 km) on the road up the valley from Abriès. This road usually has little traffic and an ascent of only 547ft (167m) is involved. It would even be possible to take a taxi from Abriès to Le Roux.

FACILITIES
Accommodation
There are gîtes d'étape at both Abriès and Le Roux. Abriès has several hotels and a dortoir (Les Edelweiss). For those taking the valley alternative there is a gîte d'étape at Ristolas.

Shops
Abriès has a full range of grocery shops, small supermarkets, bakers, butchers and shops selling fruit and vegetables and cooked meats. There is a post-office (PTT) and a bank in the town. There are no shops in Le Roux but a few of the houses offer bread, cheese and honey for sale.

Restaurants, Cafés and Bars
There are several in Abriès. There is also a restaurant in Ristolas.

Public Transport
A bus service to Château-Queyras and Montdauphin-Guillestre railway station operates from Abriès (see Appendix 2).

SUMMARY
The day begins with a steep, unrelenting climb out of the Guil Valley to the Sommet de la Lauzière. A walk along the Crête de Peyra Plata leads to the easiest summit on the whole Tour, namely the Sommet de Gilly. From here there are fine views of the Bric Bouchet, Tête du Pelvas and other peaks on the Italian border. Our route then turns back for a while to reach the border at the Col d'Urine for another look into Italy. From here there is an opportunity to climb the impressive Tête du Pelvas for a first-rate view of Monte Viso. A final descent is made through pleasant woodland to either the ski-resort of Abriès or the peaceful hamlet of Le Roux.

ROUTE
The gîte d'étape at La Monta is situated between the church and the cemetery. Take the track on the far side of the small cemetery, which soon leads to a stream (Torrent de la Chapelle). Cross this and continue, gaining height on a thin but obvious path through undergrowth to reach an area of woodland. Continue to climb through the trees. There are plenty of waymarks along this section, therefore if one is not seen for several minutes it is likely than an error has been made. This is easily done as there are many other narrow paths on this hillside. After the trees, climb through an area of rock and scrub and cross a small boulder field to reach a flatter area. Now follow a line of stakes (tipped with red and white paint) to attain the ridge, the Crête de Peyra Plata. Follow the thin but obvious path along the top of this ridge heading west to the highest point, the Sommet de la Lauzière. From here the towns of Abriès and Ristolas in the valley below can be seen.

Continue along the ridge, now called the Crête de Gilly, until a final steep descent leads to the Collette de Gilly, a pleasant spot marred only by the ski-lifts coming up from Abriès. Why this is termed a 'collette' rather than a fully grown 'col' is not altogether apparent. The rucksacks may now be left on the collette whilst the peak of the same name is claimed, 367ft above. On the summit there is a ruin of a small stone hut and a rather mysterious tall box filled with stone (there is another on the summit of Tête du Pelvas). There are views down to the hamlet of Valpréveyre and to the larger settlement of Le Roux, possibly the destination for tonight. The shapely peak to the north-east is Bric Bouchet (9,825ft/2,997m), sometimes referred to as the Matterhorn of this region. To the east is the rather evil-looking Tête du Pelvas (9,602ft/2,929m) covered in steep schist and scree slopes. To the left of the Tête du Pelvas is the Col d'Urine, the next objective of the day.

Return to the Collette de Gilly which is a good spot for lunch. There are a number of discrepancies here. First the height of the collette is given as 2,366m (7,756ft) on the map, but the signpost on the pass gives a height of 2,355m (7,720ft). Secondly, the name of the collette and peak is sometimes spelt with a G (Gilly) and sometimes with a J (Jilly). Finally, a notice-board on the collette states '1 hour 30 minutes to Valpréveyre,' whilst a second only a few yards away gives 1 hour 50 minutes to the same hamlet. Certainly an area of confusion!

The collette is also the place to take stock of the weather, the lateness of the hour and the fitness of the party. There are several options available from here. A descent can be made on the GR 58 to Ristolas to the south. Alternatively a trail can be followed towards Valpréveyre and hence down to either Le Roux or Abriès. However, if time and energy are still at hand, then the walk to the border at Col d'Urine is to be recommended for another look down into Italy.

Descend on the red/white waymarked path heading north-east towards the trees below. After about 300-400 yards the paths divide. Take the one to the left for Abriès or Le Roux, but the one to the right for the Col d'Urine (Urine is painted in yellow on the rock). After another 5 minutes or so you arrive at a wooden board at Clot Beysseys (7,333ft/2,237m). Here the GR 58 to Abriès and Le Roux is signposted to the left and the Col d'Urine and Rifugio Jervis to the right. Follow the latter path gently downhill to cross one or two small

From the Col d'Urine

streams. After the largest of these follow the waymarks to the left and across undulating ground to reach a large rock on which is a sign indicating the Col d'Urine to the right (it also bears a sign for Abriès and Le Roux back along the way just travelled and to Valpréveyre to the left). Take the good path climbing to the Col d'Urine. From here an ascent of the Tête du Pelvas may be made (see below). It is interesting to speculate on the name of this col which means exactly the same in French as it does in English!

For the descent, turn away from Italy and return to the signposted boulder referred to above. Ignore the signpost to Abriès and Le Roux, but continue down the valley following the sign to Valpréveyre. Follow both red/white and yellow waymarks to enter woodland and eventually cross a log bridge over a stream. A few yards after this, turn sharp left (do not continue ahead downhill) and climb for about 10 minutes with a stream to the left. The climb ends where the waymarked path swings to the right. Follow this to reach a sign in a clearing indicating the gîte d'étape at Abriès in 1 hour 15 minutes.

Follow this pleasant path until a major junction is reached. For Le Roux continue straight ahead on a wide track to reach the hamlet and the gîte d'étape in about 30 minutes. For Abriès turn left off this track on a path which soon joins another track. Follow this to the left (views down to Le Roux) for some way until reaching a waymarked path down to the right.

The path leads to another track where you turn right for a few yards, then left to zig-zag down to Abriès and emerge in the town to the right of the church. Turn left and, after about 150 yards, cross the bridge over the river. The gîte d'étape is then but a few yards from here. The main shops, PTT, telephone boxes etc. are in this area, the centre of the town.

ASCENT OF THE TETE DU PELVAS

From the Col d'Urine take the path heading up to the Italian side of the mountain. Soon the foot of a steep, loose gully is reached. Either climb this (danger of stone falls) or, better, tackle the scree slope a little past the gully. A cairned route should soon be picked up which leads up, steeply and unrelentingly, over rocks and boulders to the summit. The scrambling is of an easy nature, but loose in places. The top is surprisingly flat and an excellent place for a high-level picnic. The view of Monte Viso and Monte Granero and the whole Italian ridge, is perhaps, unequalled. Return to the col by the same route, taking great care to avoid creating stone falls which are the major hazard on the mountain. The peak is particularly unpleasant in this respect on fine weekends when many local hillwalkers are to be found on its slopes.

DAY 9

Le Roux or Abriès to Les Fonds de Cervières

DISTANCE			From Abriès 11.7 miles (18.8 km)				
			From Le Roux 9.3 miles (15.0 km)				
TOTAL ASCENT			From Abriès 5,203ft (1,587m)				
			From Le Roux 4,656ft (1,420m)				
TOTAL DESCENT			3,721ft (1,135m)				

	Height Above Sea Level		Ascent/Desc.		Est. Time	
					Sect.	Accum
	ft	m	ft	m	hr. m.	hr. m.
Abriès	5190	1583				
Le Roux	5737	1750	+574	+167	0.50	0.50
La Montette	6298	1921	+561	+171	0.30	1.20
Col des Thures	9169	2797	+2872	+876	2.30	3.50
Col de Rasis	9576	2921	+407	+124	0.45	4.35
Col du Malrif	9396	2866	-865	-264		
			+685	+209	1.35	6.10
Pic du Malrif	9527	2906	+131	+40	0.05	6.15
Les Fonds de Cervières	6671	2035	-2855	-871	1.50	8.05

ALTERNATIVE ROUTE FROM ABRIES TO THE COL AND
PIC DU MALRIF

DISTANCE   From Abriès to the Col du Malrif 5.7 miles

	Height Above Sea Level		Ascent/Desc.		Est. Time	
					Sect.	Accum
	ft	m	ft	m	hr m	hr m
Abriès	5190	1583				
Lac du Grand Laus	8455	2579	+3265	+996	3.30	3.30
Col du Malrif	9369	2866	+941	+287	1.00	4.30
TOTAL ASCENT			4206	1283		

Les Fonds de Cervières

THE TWO ROUTES

It is debatable which of the two routes to the Pic and Col du Malrif is the better, certainly they are very different in character. The main route described has a greater variety of scenery than the direct route and for this reason is the one recommended in this guidebook. However, after the steep climb up to the Col des Thures the route traverses some very wild and rough country before rejoining the direct route at the Col du Malrif. This part of the route is not particularly well waymarked and care is needed to maintain the correct line. The main attraction of the alternative, direct route is the idyllic Lac du Grand Laus, where a third route to the Pic and Col du Malrif is joined. This latter path is another variant of the GR 58 and ascends from Aiguilles in the south.

If starting from Abriès the main route via the Col des Thures is nearly three miles longer than the direct route, but involves less than 1,000ft (305m) of extra ascent. About 1 hour 40 minutes would be saved by taking the shorter route.

Neither route described here is advisable in adverse weather conditions and the main route via the Col des Thures and the Col de Rasis should be avoided in mist.

The alternative ascent via the Lac du Grand Laus is described at the end of the section.

FACILITIES
Accommodation
The only accommodation available after leaving Abriès or Le Roux is the gîte d'étape at Les Fonds de Cervières. This is a pleasant gîte with small rooms sleeping 6-8 people. It is open from approximately June 10th until September 11th each year.

Shops
At least three days' provisions should be purchased at Abriès. The next shop is in Brunissard (end of Day 11).

Restaurants, Cafés and Bars
There are none of these establishments until Brunissard. However, as always, the gîtes d'étape supply meals, drinks and snacks. The gîte d'étape at Les Fonds de Cervières has a bar and restaurant (open to non-residents).

Public Transport
There is none available after leaving Abriès.

SUMMARY
The highlight of today's itinerary is undoubtedly the Col and Pic du Malrif from where there is a magnificent view of the major summits of the Ecrins, some 25 miles to the north-west. The angle is such that the glaciers and snow-covered high peaks of the Ecrins are displayed more or less in a line. It is a good idea to have a small scale map of the Ecrins to help in the identification of the major summits in the massif; those with binoculars will be well rewarded!

The route descends from the Pic du Malrif down a lush valley, alongside a sparkling stream. This area is reminiscent of a typical upper mountain valley in Britain, but the illusion is broken by the presence of giant snow-capped peaks in the distance. The gîte d'étape is in amongst the wooden buildings at Les Fonds de Cervières (the head of the Cervières Valley). This tiny settlement, only inhabited during the summer months, is an area of flat, green, high Alpine pastureland.

ROUTE

From the gîte d'étape in Abriès cross the bridge over the river, turn left and walk the two miles or so along the D 441 to Le Roux. This walk is alongside the river (Torrent de Bouchet) for much of the way. There is generally little traffic along this road, particularly early in the morning. The gradient up the valley is gentle until the last few zig-zags climb steeply up to the hamlet. There are several water fountains in Le Roux from which water bottles may be filled. There is also a public telephone.

Walk through the village, pass the chapel and continue north on a good track with the river down on the left. On approaching La Montette, reach and cross a wooden footbridge spanning the river. Here is a signpost indicating the path to the Col des Thures. From here the climbing begins in earnest. The path follows a stream on the left at first and later crosses this to take a number of zig-zags up the very steep, grassy hillside. Without this well constructed path this ascent would be very laborious indeed; even so it is probably one of the hardest ascents on the whole Tour. Eventually a second notice-board is reached indicating that the walker is still en route for the correct col. This is a good spot for a rest. Continue the ascent, soon crossing a small stream, and tackle the seemingly never-ending series of zig-zags ahead as you make for the now obvious col on the skyline. The gradient does not relent until the very top is reached.

The Col des Thures is perhaps unusual in that it lacks a notice-board bearing the name of the col. There is a glorious view from here, once again on the border with Italy. The mountain to the west on the border ridge is the Grand Glaiza (10,795ft/3,293m) and the snow-covered range in the distance is the Massif des Ecrins, the Meije being the most prominent peak. This spectacular range will be seen to even better effect on the Col du Malrif (and from Pic Ouest in a few day's time).

The next section, although not technically difficult, requires some care in navigation. The area between the Col des Thures and the Col du Malrif is a rather austere, rocky wasteland. Although not to everyone's taste, it does however have a certain awe-inspiring grandeur. Take particular care not to lose the red/white waymarks which are a little thin on the ground. If the waymarks are followed and use is made of the following notes, the walker should have few problems. This stage would be difficult in mist and dangerous in wet weather because of loose schist.

Turn to the left (south-west) along the ridge, keeping to the frontier between France and Italy and following the waymarks and wooden stakes topped with red and white paint. After rounding a shoulder the Col de Rasis will be revealed ahead. It is reached by following the wooden stakes to climb up on the right side of the col (avoid veering to the left onto the scree-covered slope). The Col de Rasis (the highest col on any GR variant) lacks a notice-board but there is a red/white topped stake on its summit. Snow often remains here until late in the season.

Leave the Franco-Italian border for the last time. Descend steeply from the col over schist and scree to reach a remote tarn, unnamed on the map. On some maps the line of the GR route is shown as passing to the left (south) of this lake. This is incorrect. Locate a red/white waymark to the right of the tarn and then descend very steeply down the schist and scree of the Arête des Costetes. The route then continues across barren, open country heading in a westerly and west-south-westerly direction. There are several faint paths in this area; be sure to follow the red/white waymarkings which appear somewhat infrequently. The route maintains height for quite a while until, when the path becomes more clearly defined, it climbs over schist to gain the Crête aux Eaux Pendantes. This is followed to the Col du Malrif which is either 2,866m (9,396ft) or 2,857m (9,366ft) above sea level, depending on whether one believes the height stated on the map or that on the notice-board at the col. However both figures are higher than the 2,844m of the Col de Chamoussière, which must make the

Col du Malrif the highest col on any GR route (non-variant) within France, despite the insistence of the French authorities that the Col de Chamoussière holds this distinction.

A superb view is to be had from the Col du Malrif, but before lingering too long, climb the Pic du Malrif ahead. the extra 40m (131ft) of ascent provides an even better all-round view. This is a spot for a long rest to admire the outstanding panorama. To the west lie the snow-capped mountains of the Ecrins. From left to right the major summits are L'Ailefroide (12,959ft/3,953m), Mont Pelvoux (12,936ft/ 3,946m), Barre des Ecrins (13,447ft/4,102m) and La Meije (13,054ft/ 3,982m). A little further over to the right are the prominent Aiguilles d'Arves (11,028ft/3,364m). Much nearer than these distant giants are the Petit Rochebrune (10,091ft/3,078m) and the Pic de Rochebrune (10,884ft/3,320m). The schist and scree-covered mountain to the north is the Pic de Terre Noire on the Italian border. To the south-east Monte Viso is once again the most prominent mountain on view, and the Tête du Pelvas, Col d'Urine, La Mait d'Amunt, Bric Bouchet and Gilly are all on show. Below and to the south is the turquoise Lac du Grand Laus, passed on the direct route from Abriès. Ristolas and even L'Echalp can be seen in the valley a long way below.

Take the waymarked path steeply down from the summit of the Pic du Malrif, heading west towards the trees seen in the valley below. (Note that it is not advisable to make this descent from the Col du Malrif.) The path descends steeply over schist to reach the pasture below. From here you follow a very pleasant path down the valley with a stream (Torrent de Pierre Rouge) over to the right. Eventually the buildings of the picturesque Les Fonds (or Les Fonts) de Cervières come into view. Descend to cross a wooden footbridge and enter the hamlet.

DIRECT ROUTE FROM ABRIES TO THE COL AND PIC DU MALRIF VIA THE LAC DU GRAND LAUS

From the gîte d'étape at Abriès turn right on the road. Do not cross the bridge but, after about 50 yards, follow the red/white waymarks to the right to climb the hill and pass the small church (this is floodlit at night and is a very attractive feature on the hillside). Pass the deserted hamlet of Le Malrif and after a while reach a stream (Torrent du Malrif). Follow this until a bridge is reached at the Bergerie des Bertins (6,688ft/2,040m). Continue on a good path to climb steeply to the Lac du Grand Laus. The path passes to the east of the tarn and then continues to climb towards the north, aiming for the Crête aux Eaux Pendantes and the Pic and Col du Malrif. There is a good waymarked path all the way.

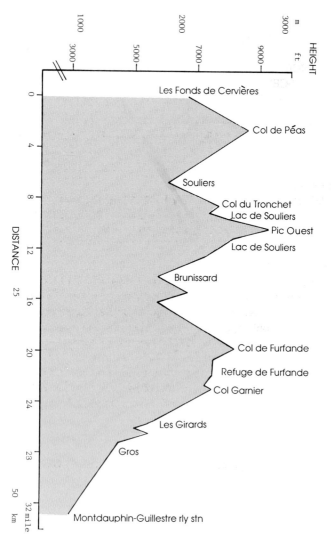

PROFILE OF DAYS 10-13

Les Fonds de Cervières to Souliers

DISTANCE	6.7 miles (10.8 km)
TOTAL ASCENT	2,111ft (644m)
TOTAL DESCENT	2,738ft (835m)

	Height Above Sea Level		Ascent/Desc.		Est. Time	
					Sect.	Accum
	ft	m	ft	m	hr m	hr m
Les Fonds de Cervières	6671	2035				
Col de Péas	8619	2629	+2111	+644		
			-164	-50	2.20	2.20
Souliers	6045	1844	-2574	-785	2.10	4.30

OPTIONAL EXCURSIONS

A visit to the town of Château-Queyras is well worthwhile. This stage is only a short one and so plenty of time should be available for a visit to the town if desired. The fort at Château-Queyras, dating from the 13th century, is only open to visitors during July and August. The opening times are normally 2.00-6.00 p.m. every day except Tuesday. The town has numerous facilities (see below) and several souvenir shops. Château-Queyras can be reached either by a footpath which leaves the main route before the hamlet of Souliers, or by one of two minor roads from Souliers. Both are indicated in the route description.

FACILITIES

Accommodation

There is a gîte d'étape at Souliers. There are hotels at Château-Queyras.

Shops

The only shops are those off-route at Château-Queyras.

Restaurants, Cafés and Bars

Once again these are only to be found in Château-Queyras.

Public Transport

A bus service operates from Château-Queyras to Abriès or to the Montdauphin-Guillestre railway station (see Appendix 2).

SUMMARY

Today's journey is a short one, allowing for a half-day rest after the rigours of the last few days. There are several ways in which to spend the day. An extended picnic lunch on the Col de Péas may be attractive for some, whilst the more active may wish to go off-route to explore the ancient asbestos mine workings below the col. Perhaps the most rewarding excursion is that to Château-Queyras for a visit to the old fort.

There is but one climb on the route and this is only a 2,000ft (610m) ascent to the Col de Péas. The way is straightforward and should present no difficulties.

It is perfectly possible to combine Days 10 and 11 into one long walk, particularly if the detour to Lac de Souliers and Pic Ouest is omitted. (see Day 11).

ROUTE

From the gîte d'étape at Les Fonds, return to the wooden bridge to cross the river and head south with a gorge on the right. Pass a waterfall over on the right. Later the path descends a little to cross the river. From here climb the shoulder to the right of the col seen ahead. On reaching this shoulder the path flattens a little before a final climb to the Col de Péas. A board on the col indicates the GR 58 to Souliers (2 hours 30 minutes) and to Les Meyries (3 hours). There is also a fingerpost indicating a route to the Pic de Rochebrune (10,884ft/ 3,320m) but the ascent from the col does not look particularly easy.

The descent from the Col de Péas is a delight. Descend south on the path. This soon follows a stream for a while. The area was once mined for asbestos and the ancient mines can be examined (with care) by following a detour off the main path (marked on the 1:25,000 IGN map).

For Souliers, follow red and white tipped wooden stakes to contour around the hillside. Eventually a signpost is reached indicating Meyries and Château-Queyras straight ahead on a footpath down the hillside. If wishing to visit Château-Queyras (4,426ft/1,350m) this path can be recommended. For a return to Souliers from Château-Queyras the GR 5 can be taken to the artificial Lac de Roue (the route is marked on IGN maps), then the minor road followed north to Souliers. However for the direct route to Souliers turn right at the signpost and contour around the hillside with views of the wooded, steep-sided valley below. Eventually the path drops steeply to reach a large wooden cross (Croix de Souliers). Take the path to the right of this to descend to Souliers. On entering the hamlet pass to the right of 'Le Grand Rochebrun' and walk down a stepped street to the gîte d'étape (GTA) on the road.

It is possible to make a circular excursion from Souliers to Château-Queyras. For the outward journey take the road/dirt track from the small chapel in Souliers to the Lac de Roue. From here join the GR 5 and descend, following red/white waymarks to Château-Queyras. The descent is gentle at first but then the path drops more steeply to arrive at the D 947 road. Turn left here to enter the town. A return can be made either by the same route, or alternatively by a road climbing to the north-west from Château-Queyras directly to Souliers. The round trip takes about 3-4 hours walking time. Remember Château-Queyras at 4,426ft (1,350m) is much lower than Souliers (6,045ft/1,844m), so 1,619ft (494m) of descent and re-ascent is involved.

DAY 11

Souliers to Brunissard via the Lac de Souliers

DISTANCE   7.4 miles (11.9 km)
TOTAL ASCENT   3,606ft (1,100m)
TOTAL DESCENT   3,927ft (1,198m)

	Height Above Sea Level		Ascent/Desc.		Est. Time	
					Sect.	Accum
	ft	m	ft	m	hr m	hr m
Souliers	6045	1844				
Col du Tronchet	7694	2347	+1649	+503	1.25	1.25
Lac de Souliers	8169	2492	-328	-100		
			+803	+245	1.00	2.25
Pic Ouest	9323	2844	+1154	+352	0.55	3.20
Lac de Souliers	8169	2492	-1154	-352	0.35	3.55
Road (D 902)	7212	2200	-957	-292	0.50	4.45
Brunissard	5724	1746	-1488	-454	0.50	5.35

OPTIONAL EXCURSIONS

The excursion to the Lac de Souliers and the ascent of Pic Ouest are both off-route and could be omitted by those intent only on the shortest route between the two villages. However both are recommended and as the stage is quite short there should be ample time to include both of them in the itinerary. Note that the climb to Pic Ouest from the lakeside should not be attempted in bad weather.

FACILITIES

Accommodation

There is a gîte d'étape (Les Bons Enfants) at Brunissard where excellent hospitality is to be found. The hamlet of La Chalp, 1 mile south of Brunissard, has a hotel which also has a dortoir (see Appendix 1 for details).

Shops
There is an épicerie in Brunissard, a short walk from the gîte d'étape in the centre of the village. A comprehensive range of fresh fruit, vegetables, cooked meats and bread is stocked, as well as the usual grocery items.

Restaurants, Cafés and Bars
The gîte d'étape in Brunissard also functions as a restaurant and bar. The food is recommended.

Public Transport
There is no public transport. A taxi may be hired from Brunissard.

SUMMARY
The highlight of this stage is the detour to the Lac de Souliers. Surrounded by spectacular rocky mountains, the lake is a superb setting for a long picnic lunch. Those with more energy will want to climb the nearby Pic Ouest. Although steep, it is not a difficult climb and views from the summit of the mountains of the Ecrins and the Vanoise are magnificent.

ROUTE
Head north from the gîte d'étape at Souliers, soon passing a small chapel on the left (turn left here for the Lac de Roue and Château-Queyras). Keep straight on heading north with a river to the left (Torrent de Souliers). The track is fairly level. Avoid crossing any of the numerous wooden footbridges over the river until a red and white sign indicates the correct one to be taken. Once over the river the track begins to climb towards the chalet with a wooden verandah which is seen up ahead. Pass to the right of this building and soon begin to zig-zag up to the col to the west. After passing through an area of patchy fir trees the Col du Tronchet is soon attained. It is not a long or difficult climb. There are views from here down into the wide, fertile valley in which Brunissard is situated.

The path descends a little over to the right (north-west) and

The Brunissard valley from the Col du Tronchet

undulates across the hillside for a while. In about ¹/₃ of a mile (0.5 km) a short, steep ascent is reached. About 150 yards after the top of this climb a rock is passed which bears the words 'Col du Tronchet' and an arrow pointing back to the south-east. About 50 yards after this, bear to the right (north-east) to climb over undulating ground to pick up a minor path. (If you are omitting the detour to the Lac de Souliers, remain on the main path to descend to Brunissard.) Climb on the well-worn path to reach the Lac de Souliers. On the way an area of stone writing (words created with letters constructed using small rocks or stones) is passed. The Lac de Souliers is in a glorious position with the jagged Crête des Oules to the north-east and Pic Ouest (perhaps not surprisingly) to the west. On the north bank of the lake will be seen other examples of stone writing. Many of the well known French cities have been spelled out with rocks on the grass, including Paris, Rennes, Caen and Tours. There is even a large 'Vive La France!' The lake is a good spot to sunbathe and generally relax, but a paddle is not recommended for the water is usually icy-cold, whatever the weather, and the bed of the lake drops away very steeply.

The more energetic will wish to make an ascent of Pic Ouest, the path for which can be seen leading up from the west end of the lake. Walk to the end of the lake and climb over a series of hillocks to locate the thin but obvious path. Gain height on this, heading towards the ridge ahead. Cross an area of scree and pass to the right of a large depression to gain the lowest point of the ridge. Turn left here and climb to the summit where there is a cairn and a glorious all-round view. The peaks and glaciers of the Ecrins are particularly well displayed and there is another opportunity to see the very familiar shape of Monte Viso. The glacier-covered mountain to the north is the Grande Casse (12,657ft/3,861m) in the Vanoise. The valley leading to Briançon is also visible from here. The ridge can be followed from the cairn to its southernmost point by following a line of red paint stripes. At the south peak there is the equivalent of a British trig. point. Return to the Lac de Souliers by the route of ascent.

Descend from the Lac de Souliers by the same route to re-join the GR 58 and resume the descent to Brunissard. Descend on the path through woodland to meet a road (the D 902). Cross this to find another path heading down into woodland. Descend, noting the enormous scree slopes above, to a small stream. Do not cross this at once but turn left instead and cross it some 150 yards further on. Notice the strangely eroded cliffs of gypsum to the left. Descend with a (usually) dry stream bed on the left, later crossing this and descending with the stream bed on the right to reach a track which passes through an area of holiday homes (strange looking buildings built on tall, concrete pillars). The track descends to a road (the D 902 again) where there is a footpath sign indicating the Col d'Izoard, a major road pass in the area which allows access into the Queyras from the Briançon Valley.

For Brunissard, turn right on the D 902 for about 300 yards, then a few yards past the sign for Brunissard on the roadside, turn right for the gîte d'étape which is located about 100 yards along this street on the right-hand side. The épicerie is found by continuing along the D 902 to the telephone box where you turn right. Follow the signs to the

The summit of Pic Ouest

épicerie (about 70 yards from the telephone box). The shop opens from 7.00 a.m. until late. Ring the bell if it appears closed (it rarely is!).

View of the distant Écrins from the summit of Pic Ouest (Day 11)

The Lac de Souliers and the Crête du Tronchet (Day 11)

Furfande from the Col de Furfande (Refuge is the most distant building) (Day 12).

Chalets and mountains at Furfande (Day 1 and Day 13)

DAY 12

Brunissard to Furfande

DISTANCE   6.5 miles (10.5 km)
TOTAL ASCENT   3,455ft (1,054m)
TOTAL DESCENT   1,662ft (507m)

	Height Above Sea Level		Ascent/Desc.		Est. Time	
					Sect.	Accum
	ft	m	ft	m	hr m	hr m
Brunissard	5724	1746				
Col de Furfande	8196	2500	+3455	+1054		
			-983	-300	4.45	4.45
Refuge de Furfande	7517	2293	-679	-207	0.25	5.10

ALTERNATIVE ROUTES

Brunissard is a meeting point for two GR routes, the GR 58 and the GR 5. An alternative to the route described here (the GR 58) is to take the GR 5 south to Ceillac, from where a bus may be taken to Montdauphin-Guillestre railway station. The route, marked on the IGN and Didier and Richard maps, goes via La Chalp, Les Maisons, Lac de Roue, Château-Queyras and Col Fromage (7,543ft/2,301m) to Ceillac. Walking time is about 8 hours with approximately 3,144ft (959m) of ascent. The section from Château-Queyras to Ceillac via Col Fromage is particularly fine. Another alternative is to follow the GR 5 north over the Col des Ayes to Briançon (about 5 hours and 2,396ft, 731m of ascent). Although the city of Briançon is well worth a visit (see Day 13) the final stages of the GR 5 into Briançon are not particularly pleasant.

FACILITIES
Accommodation
The Refuge de Furfande is the only possibility for overnight accommodation. The resident guardian provides dinner and breakfast, but only from the beginning of July until the end of the first week in September. Outside this period accommodation is provided (free of charge) in a small winter room which is part of the refuge.

Shops
There are no shops until reaching the Durance Valley at the end of the Tour. Therefore it is necessary to carry food for lunches etc. from Brunissard.

Restaurants, Cafés and Bars
None are passed on the route.

Public Transport
No public transport is available.

SUMMARY
For those with plenty of energy but a shortage of time it is possible to combine the last two days and reach the Durance Valley in one long day. However, this is a tiring and lengthy walk and would leave little time for savouring the scenery or for exploring Guillestre and Montdauphin at the end of the day. It is therefore more sensible, if time permits, to stay a second night at the Refuge de Furfande. The climb to the Col de Furfande is a long one involving sections of ascent and descent before the final lengthy haul up to the col. Furfande is such a lush, verdant place amidst grand scenery, that a second night here is definitely no hardship!

Note that after leaving Brunissard the first mile or two described in this guidebook is not the official route of the GR 58. Although there is somewhat more ascent and descent involved in the described route, it is preferable to the GR 58 which stays lower in the valley before finally climbing.

ROUTE
On leave the gîte d'étape at Brunissard, turn right and pass under the

wooden bridge over the street. At the T-junction at the edge of the hamlet turn right and, after some 150 yards, left over a footbridge. In a few yards a signpost will be reached indicating a forest track to Le Coin and La Chalp (a yellow walking man symbol). Climb gradually at first, then more steeply towards the south on this forest track with views down left to the valley floor below. The track eventually takes a wide sweep to the left and descends a little. About 250 yards before the track comes to an abrupt end, locate a fingerpost indicating Le Coin and La Chalp down on a thin path to the left. Take this path to follow a succession of similar fingerposts. The path zig-zags downhill, eventually meeting the official red/white waymarked route which joins from the left. Turn right here and follow the waymarks descending to a plank footbridge.

Cross the bridge and follow the GR 58/Le Lauzon sign to the right. After about 150 yards take the GR 58 sign to the left (the Le Lauzon route crosses the river to the right). Climb on a series of zig-zags through woodland. After this ascent the path contours a little and then descends somewhat, passing through sections of woodland and over areas of scree, eventually reaching a (usually) dry river bed. Cross this and shortly reach and cross a mountain stream. Here there is a signpost indicating Brunissard (2 hours) back along the path. Turn right on the track here and in 30 yards take another (upper) track to the right. Follow this as it zig-zags uphill heading towards the col. Cut the zig-zags on this track several times by following path shortcuts. This track is motorable and is the means by which supplies are taken to the Col de Furfande for the Refuge de Furfande, 679ft (207m) below the col. Continue upwards, passing a memorial cross, to meet a stream. Follow this uphill, first on its left and later crossing over to climb to its right. In the latter stages of the climb the track swings far over to the right, but the waymarked footpath climbs more steeply, the two meeting just before the Col de Furfande.

There are extensive views from the col. Look down on the chalets and the refuge, last visited twelve days ago. It is somewhat irritating after the rigours of the climb to find a small car park at the col! There is a large wooden cross on the col and also a signpost pointing back

On the approach to the Col de Furfande

to Arvieux (reached in 2 hours 30 minutes). The GR 541 joins the GR 58 at the Col de Furfande. Those staying the night at the refuge should first take the path heading down to the right, but after about 100 yards turn left at a signposted rock to follow the GR 58 down to the Refuge de Furfande seen below. Those continuing to the Durance Valley should take the GR 541 meandering down the hillside to reach the Chalets de Furfande, then rejoin the route used in the ascent at the beginning of the Tour.

DAY 13

Furfande to the Durance Valley

DISTANCE   12.2 miles (19.6 km)
TOTAL ASCENT   731ft (223m)
TOTAL DESCENT   5,298ft (1,616m)

	Height Above Sea Level		Ascent/Desc.		Est. Time	
					Sect.	Accum
	ft	m	ft	m	hr m	hr m
Refuge de Furfande	7517	2293				
Les Granges de Furfande	7474	2280	-43	-13	0.25	0.25
Col Garnier	7470	2279	-243	-74		
			+239	+73	0.50	1.15
Les Girards	5475	1670	-1996	- 609	1.35	2.50
Gros	4540	1385	-1426	- 435		
			+492	+150	1.15	4.05
Montdauphin	3459	1055	-1082	-330	1.10	5.15
Montdauphin-Guillestre . Rly. Stn	2950	900	-508	-155	0.35	5.50

OPTIONAL EXCURSION

For those wanting to bag a final peak, the summit of Garnier can be climbed from just below Col Garnier.

ALTERNATIVE ROUTES

The obvious alternative to the described route is to take the GR 541 variant to the Durance Valley via Col Saint-Antoine and the Col de Moussiere, i.e. the reverse of Day 1.

On today's route there are four possible destinations after passing the hamlet of Gros:

(1)   Eygliers and a direct descent to the Montdauphin-Guillestre

133

railway station.

(2)   Eygliers followed by a visit to the fortified town of Montdauphin before descending to the railway station.

(3)   Guillestre via La Font d'Eygliers. A bus can be taken from Guillestre to the Montdauphin-Guillestre railway station (see Appendix 2).

(4)   Le Coin and the GR 541 to Saint-Crépin. This is the most pleasant of the four routes being mainly along forest tracks (see Day 1, Alternative Start). Those with more holiday remaining may wish to continue on the GR 541 to join the GR 54 (Tour de l'Oisans) at the Pas de la Cavale for a circuit of the Ecrins National Park. For those returning to Montdauphin-Guillestre railway station there is an unpleasant $2^1/4$ mile (3.6 km) walk south along the busy N 94 from Saint-Crépin; a taxi may be preferable.

All four above routes are marked on the IGN maps.

FACILITIES
Refer to Day 1.

SUMMARY
The last day is nearly all descent, leaving the high mountains and returning to the Durance Valley. The route crosses the high Alpine pasture of Furfande and climbs to the 21st and last col included in this Tour, Col Garnier. Here is the place for an extended 'elevenses,' looking out over the mountains of the Queyras and the country that has been explored for the last 13 days. It is a time for reflection and for planning the next trip to the Alps. The long descent that follows is a touch hard on the knees, but this will be of little consequence at this late stage in the Tour.

There are a number of possibilities for sightseeing at the end of the holiday, including Guillestre, Montdauphin and particularly Briancon. These towns are briefly described at the end.

ROUTE
From the Refuge de Furfande retrace the route of the GR 541 taken on

On the descent from Col Garnier

Day 1, passing through the area of scattered chalets. The multitude
of paths at Furfande makes the route a little confusing, but the way
should never really be in doubt as the grassy Col Garnier should be
clearly visible ahead. Descend past the chalets heading towards the
scree slopes beneath the crags to the west. On approaching these
scree slopes pick up the main path heading south to reach the notice-
board and division of paths at the place referred to as Panneau on the
IGN maps. It is here where the GR 541 variant from Col Saint-Antoine
(see Day 1) meets the GR 541 from Col Garnier. Take the GR 541
heading south. Follow the path which climbs the grassy slopes to
reach Col Garnier. There is an old notice-board here showing the col
to have a height of 2,280m (7,474ft).

Col Garnier is a beautiful spot for a long stop and look back down
over the lush green of Furfande to the rocky ridges above. Note the
Refuge de Furfande, the large building on the extreme right.
Peakbaggers may fancy climbing Garnier itself. This can be done by
first avoiding the rocky spur on the ridge to the west, best achieved

The Gorges du Guil and the Guil valley

by descending south from the col for a few yards then heading upwards and aiming for the ridge north of the peak. From here the summit of Garnier (7,973ft/2,432m) should be easily attained (note that the author has not ascended this peak).

Take a last look at the mountains of the Queyras before descending south from Col Garnier over a grassy area on a thin path. Eventually this enters woodland and descends more steeply with views down to the Combe de Queyras. The way is rather pleasant with several sunny glades amongst the trees. At 1,750m (5,737ft) notice the sign 'abri' pointing to the right. This refers to a small shelter. To reach it climb steeply to the right for 100 yards to locate the cabin next to a ruined bar (neither buildings are visible from the GR 541). The shelter has a table, stove and sleeping area suitable for two people. It would be a haven in bad weather. Back on the GR 541 continue downhill through woodland to reach the ruined buildings of Les Girards. Here is a sign indicating the way to Gros (1 hour) and Eygliers (2 hours). Now the route heads towards the west, descending steeply to a plank bridge over a river (Torrent de la Valette). Soon after this there is a short, steep climb with a gorge dropping precipitously on the left (take care). The path levels, passes under electricity cables close to a large pylon on the left and continues on a track, eventually reaching a minor road just before the hamlet of Gros. There is a signpost here (Font d'Eygliers 1 hour) indicating a turn to the left to enter Gros. Ignore this and continue instead on the surfaced road. This is a minor road, usually carrying little traffic. There are superb views to the left down into the Gorges du Guil. The Durance Valley is spread out below, the river flowing to Guillestre and Montdauphin with its fort clearly visible. The snow-covered mountains ahead are those of the Ecrins, with Mont Pelvoux the most prominent peak. Eventually a sign is reached indicating the GR 541 variant via the Col de Moussière on the Route Forestière de Bois Durat on the right. There are several choices of route from here (see Alternative Routes above).

GUILLESTRE

To reach Guillestra descend by a minor road to La Font d'Eygliers and continue to cross the bridge over the River Guil to enter the town. Here there are many cafés and restaurants, souvenir shops, banks, hotels and a youth hostel. Guillestre is on the edge of three regions; the Queyras, Haute Ubaye and Embrunais. Haute Ubaye in particular is an area worthy of exploration if time is available.

Guillestre is the largest town in the Queyras but even so it only has a population of about 2,000. It acts as a gateway into the Queyras being situated at the south-western corner of the region, close to where the Guil and Durance valleys converge. It boasts an interesting 16th century church with columns and crouching lions of marble at the entrance.

EYGLIERS AND MONTDAUPHIN

Descend by minor road to the village of Eygliers, noting the impressive sundial on the church. Continue on the road to cross the moat and two drawbridges guarding the entrance to the fortified town of Montdauphin.

The town stands on a high natural outcrop of rock above the Durance Valley. It was constructed on the orders of Louis XIV in 1693 at a time when France was at war with the independent state of Savoie (Savoy). Château-Queyras and Briancon were fortified during the same period. There is a military presence even to this day and the town appears rather stark and austere, despite the presence of an artisan area. There is a post office (PTT), an épicerie, bar, hotel, café and restaurant. The railway station of Montdauphin-Guillestre, near to the confluence of the Guil and the Durance, is easily reached by a short road walk (or taxi) from Montdauphin.

BRIANÇON

Briançon is strictly outside the Queyras region but can easily be reached by a short train journey from Montdauphin-Guillestre railway station. A day trip here is highly recommended. There is a direct train service from Briançon to Paris (see Appendix 2).

The ancient city of Briançon has a rich and varied history. The old town was built for defensive purposes on a massive rock outcrop overlooking several major valley systems. It was further fortified with battlements, a city wall and army barracks since it occupied such a strategically important position, guarding the Col de Montgenèvre into Italy. There was a very large garrison stationed here during the First World War and in earlier times the fortress town was involved in campaigns with the neighbouring region of Savoie. (Further details of the long history of Briançon can be obtained at the spectacular son et lumière held on the walls of the citadel on most evenings from around mid-July until mid-August. This show is highly recommended although, of course, the documentary is given in French.)

The city has now greatly expanded outside the ancient city walls. Today it is the major commercial, industrial and administrative centre for the region. It is the highest city of its size in France (4,229ft/ 1,290m); only Davos in Switzerland is higher in all Europe. Briançon is also famous for its sundials of which there are numerous splendid examples to be seen on the walls of many of its old buildings.

Briançon

There is a gîte d'étape at Fontenil, about 25 minutes walk to the north-east of Briançon, and the city has an abundance of shops, cafés, restaurants and hotels. There is a bank, a post office (PTT) and a tourist office. Apart from the trains there are bus services to Bourg d'Oisans, Grenoble, Gap and Chambéry.

APPENDIX 1

List of Refuges and Gîtes d'Etape in the Queyras and Neighbouring Regions

Establishments listed in brackets do not lie directly on the route of the walking Tour.

GTA = Grande Traversée des Alpes, an organisation which operates a system of gîtes d'étape in the French Alps.

CAF = Club Alpin Français.

CAI = Club Alpin Italiano.

1.   EYGLIERS
Gîte d'Etape d'Eygliers. GTA. Half a mile north-west of the Montdauphin-Guillestre railway station in the Durance Valley (*not* in the village of Eygliers). 30 places. Meals available. Tel 92.45.12.29.

2.   GUILLESTRE
[Youth Hostel. 80 places. Meals available. Tel 92.45.04.32.]

3.   FURFANDE
Refuge de Furfande. GTA. Below the Col de Furfande. 25 places. Guardian in summer only. Meals available. No telephone.

4.   MONTBARDON
[Gîte d'Etape de Montbardon. GTA. 27 places. Meals available. Tel 92.45.70.78.]

5.   CEILLAC
Gîte d'Etape de Ceillac. Les Baladins. GTA. 70 places. Meals available. Tel 92.45.00.23.

6.   CIME DU MELEZET
[Gîte d'Etape de la Cîme du Mélezet. 2 miles (3.2 km) south-east of Ceillac. 15 places. Meals available. Tel 92.45.19.12.]

7.   LE RAUX
Dortoir. Half a mile (0.8 km) below Saint-Véran. Rooms for 2 and 4 persons.

8. SAINT-VERAN

Gîte d'Etape de Saint-Véran. Le Chant de L'Alpe. GTA. 50 places. Meals available. Tel 92.45.82.19.

9. SAINT-VERAN

Gîte d'Etape de Saint-Véran. Les Gabelous. 40 places. Meals available. Open all year. Tel 92.45.81.39.

10. LA BLANCHE

[Refuge de la Blanche. By the Lac de la Blanche. Three-quarters of a mile (1.2 km) north-west of Col Blanchet. 20 places. Guardian in summer only. Meals available. Tel 92.45.81.33.]

11. AGNEL

Refuge Agnel. GTA. Half a mile (0.8 km) north-west of Col Agnel. 80 places. Guardian from mid-June to mid-September and during the winter skiing season. Meals available. Tel 92.45.83.96.

12. MOLINES-EN-QUEYRAS

[Gîte d'Etape de Molines-en-Queyras. Lou Barmiane. 18 places. Meals available. Tel 92.45.81.16.]

13. VILLE-VIEILLE

[Gîte d'Etape de Ville-Vieille. 18 places. Open summer only. Meals available. Tel 92.45.70.82.]

14. CHIANALE

[Gîte d'Etape Chianale (Italy). 28 places. Open March to September. Meals available. Tel 0175 950189.]

15. GAGLIARDONE

[Rifugio Gagliardone. CAI. In the upper Vallanta Valley, Italy. 32 places. Guardian during the summer months. Meals available. Tel 0175 95183]

16. VALLANTA

[Rifugio Vallanta. CAI. In the upper Vallanta Valley, Italy. Half a mile south of the Rifugio Gagliardone. 84 places. Guardian during the summer months. Meals available. No telephone.]

17. VISO

Refuge de Baillif-Viso. CAF. In the upper Guil Valley. 40 places. Guardian in spring and summer only. Meals available. Tel 92.45.75.66

or 92.45.72.26.

18.   GRANERO

Rifigio Granero. CAI. In the upper Pellice Valley, Italy. 52 places. Guardian from July to September. Meals available. No telephone.

19.   JERVIS

Rifugio Jervis. CAI. In the Pellice Valley, Italy. 150 places. Guardian from May to October. Meals available. Tel 0121 92811.

20.   LA MONTA

Gîte d'Etape La Monta. In the upper Guil Valley. 48 places. Guardian during the summer and the winter skiing season. Meals available. Tel 92.45.71.35.

21.   RISTOLAS

[Gîte d'Etape de Ristolas. Les Eterlous de Lestio. Opened July, 1988. Dormitories for between 4 and 8 persons. Tel 92.45.76.07.]

22.   ABRIES

Gîte d'Etape d'Abriès. 50 places. Meals available. Tel 92.45.71.14.

23.   LE ROUX

Gîte d'Etape du Roux d'Abriès. 50 places. Meals available. Tel 92.45.74.30.

24.   LES FONDS DE CERVIERES

Refuge Les Fonds de Cervières. 60 places. Guardian in summer only. Meals available. Tel 92.21.32.82.

25.   SOULIERS

Gîte d'Etape de Souliers. GTA. 60 places. Meals available. Tel 92.45.75.55 or 92.45.76.90.

26.   BRUNISSARD

Gîte d'Etape de Brunissard. 24 places. Meals available. Tel 92.45.73.85.

27.   LA CHALP

[Hotel La Borne Ensoleillée. 1 mile (1.6 km) south of Brunissard. Dortoir. 16 places. Open summer only. Meals available. Tel 92.45.72.89.]

28.   BRIANÇON

[Gîte d'Etape de Briançon. At Fontenil, 1 mile (1.6 km) north-east of the centre of Briançon. 49 places. Meals available. Tel 92.21.28.93.]

APPENDIX 2

Local Bus and Train Services

A.   BUS SERVICES

The following bus services were operating in the Queyras during the summer of 1988. Note that the timetables given refer to the July/ August service only; there is a much inferior service after the first week in September. The timing and availability of services are subject to change from year to year, but these tables do give an indication of the services that will probably be available, the times between destinations and the frequency of the buses. The services are daily (24 hour clock).

(1)   **Montdauphin-Guillestre Railway Station to Ceillac**

7.55	9.55	17.20	Montdauphin-G. Rly. Stn.
8.25	10.45	17.50	Ceillac
Return:			
7.00	8.45	16.00	Ceillac
7.30	9.15	16.30	Montdauphin-G. Rly. Stn.

(2)   **Montdauphin-Guillestre Railway Station to Guillestre and Vars les Claux**

	7.55	17.20	Montdauphin-G. Rly. Stn.
	8.00		Guillestre
	8.30	18.00	Vars les Claux
Return:			
	9.15	18.25	Vars les Claux
	9.45	19.00	Guillestre
	10.55	19.10	Montdauphin-G. Rly. Stn.

(3)   **Montdauphin-Guillestre Railway Station to Château-Queyras and Abriès**

7.55	17.20	Montdauphin-G. Rly. Stn.

8.45	15.00	18.10	Château-Queyras
9.00	15.15	18.25	Abriès
Return:			
10.00	15.20	18.40	Abriès
10.20	15.35	19.00	Château-Queyras
10.55	16.30	19.40	Montdauphin-G. Rly. Stn.

B.   TRAIN SERVICES

There are trains from Montdauphin-Guillestre to L'Argentière-la-Bessée (15 minutes) and Briançon (30 minutes) about six times a day. Trains to Embrun (20 minutes), Gap (1 hour), Veynes-Dévoluy (1 hour 30 minutes), Die (2 hours 45 minutes), Crest (3 hours 15 minutes) and Valence (4 hours) also operate about six times per day.

APPENDIX 3

List of Cols and Summits on the
Tour of the Queyras

	COL	HEIGHT ABOVE SEA LEVEL		DATE ASCENDED	COMMENTS
		ft	m		
1.	Col de Moussière	7717	2354		
2.	Col Saint-Antoine	8058	2458		
3.	Col de Bramousse	7379	2251		
4.	[Col Fromage]	7543	2301		
5.	Col des Estronques	8691	2651		
6.	Col de Saint-Véran	9323	2844		
7.	Col de Chamoussière	9323	2844		
8.	Col Vieux	9199	2806		
9.	Col Agnel	8996	2744		
10.	Passo della Losetta	9409	2870		
11.	Col Valante	9228	2815		
12.	Col Sellière	9291	2834		
13.	Col Lacroix	7537	2299		
14.	Collette de Gilly	7756	2366		
15.	Col d'Urine	8278	2525		
16.	Col des Thures	9169	2797		
17.	Col de Rasis	9576	2921		
18.	Col du Malrif	9396	2866		
19.	Col de Péas	8619	2629		
20.	Col du Tronchet	7694	2347		
21.	Col de Furfande	8196	2500		
22.	Col Garnier	7471	2279		

	PEAK	HEIGHT ABOVE SEA LEVEL		DATE ASCENDED	COMMENTS
		ft	m		
A.	Tête de Jacquette	9038	2757		
B.	Pic de Caramantran	9917	3025		
C.	Le Pain de Sucre	10517	3208		
D.	Pointe Joanne	10005	3052		
E.	Monte Granero	10379	3166		
F.	Sommet de la Lauzière	8445	2576		
G.	Sommet de Gilly	8088	2467		
H.	La Mait d'Amunt	9192	2804		
I.	Tête du Pelvas (Mon Palavas)	9602	2929		
J.	Pic du Malrif	9527	2906		
K.	Pic Ouest	9323	2844		
L.	Garnier	7973	2432		

APPENDIX 4

Bibliography

1.   *Off the Beaten Track - France.* Edited by Martin Collins (1988). Moorland Publishing Company. Includes a chapter on touring and walking in the Queyras. Written for the adventurous tourist. Good background reading.

2.   *Walking in France* by Rob Hunter (1982). Oxford Illustrated Press (Hardback) or Hamlyn Paperback edition (1983). Useful information on all aspects of walking in France.

3.   *Hannibal's Footsteps* by Bernard Levin (1985). Jonathan Cape. The story of a modern day walk made by the author (with a film crew of six others) along one of the possible routes taken by Hannibal and his elephants on their journey across Europe in 218BC. A trail was followed across France from the Camargue, via the Rhône Valley and over the Alps into Italy. The final stages of the trek were in the Queyras. A night was spent in the Refuge Agnel before crossing over into Italy via the Col Agnel. The text is of the usual high quality expected of this renowned author and journalist.

4.   *Walking the French Alps: GR 5* by Martin Collins (1984). Cicerone Press. The guidebook to the Grande Taversée des Alpes which passes through the Queyras.

5.   *Tour of the Oisans: GR 54* by Andrew Harper (1986). Cicerone Press. A circular walk around the Dauphiné Alps (Ecrins).

6.   *100 Hikes in the Alps* by Ira Spring and Harvey Edwards (1979). Published by The Mountaineers, USA. Includes a walk in the Queyras and details of the Italian Mon Viso Tour.

7.   *Walking Europe from Top to Bottom* by Susanna Margolis and Ginger Harmon (1986). Sierra Club Books, San Francisco. Includes an account of a walk through the Queyras on the GR 5.

8.   *Backpacking and Walking in Italy* by Stefano Ardito (1987). Bradt Publications. Includes details of the Mon Viso Tour.

9.   *Michelin Green Guide - Alpes du Sud*. Michelin Tyre Company, France. In French. Contains a section on the Queyras. General tourist information.

10.   *Gîtes d'Etape de Randonnée et Refuges*. France and Frontières by Annick & Serge Mouraret. 3rd Edition (1988). Creer. Lists some 2,900 establishments including all those in the Queyras and neighbouring Italian Alps.

APPENDIX 5

Useful Addresses

1.   French Government Tourist Office: 178 Piccadilly, London W1V 0AL. Tel (01) 493 3371.

2.   Parc Natural Régional du Queyras: Avenue de la Gare, B.P. 3. 05600, Guillestre, Haute-Alpes. France.

3.   Edward Stanford Ltd. (specialist map shop): 12-14 Long Acre, London WC2E 9LP. Tel (01) 836 1321.

4.   McCarta Ltd. (specialist map shop): 122 Kings Cross Road, London WC1X 9DS.

5.   The Map Shop: 15 High Street, Upton-upon-Severn, Worcestershire WR8 0HJ.

6.   Au Vieux Campeur: 48 Rue Des Ecoles, 75005 Paris. Nearest métro station is Maubert-Mutaulité. Extensive range of French maps and guidebooks.

7.   IGN Shop: 107 Rue la Boétie, 75008 Paris. Just off the Champs-Elysées. Nearest métro station is Georges V. Complete range of IGN maps of France at 1:50,000 and 1:25,000.

8.   CIMES: Maison du Tourisme, 14 Rue de la Republique, 38019 Grenoble, France. Ask for an up-to-date list of all the gîtes d'étape and refuges in the Queyras.

9.   British Airways London Reservation Centre: P.O. Box 10, Heathrow Airport (London) Hounslow TW6 2JA. Information on relevant flights to the area.

10.   Falcon Holidays (for charter flights to Geneva and Nice): 33 Notting Hill Gate, London W11 3JQ. Tel London 01-221 0088 or Manchester 061-831 7000 or Birmingham 021-233 3131 or Glasgow 041-204 0242.

11.   National Express Coach Service: Eurolines, Victoria Coach Station, London SW1. Tel 01 730 0202.

12.   British Mountaineering Council (BMC): Crawford House, Precinct Centre, Booth Street East, Manchester M13 9RZ. The BMC will provide information on the following:

(i)   Overseas insurance schemes for mountaineers, climbers, hillwalkers and ramblers.

(ii)   The Reciprocal Rights Card which entitles the holder to discount rates in Alpine huts (refuges).

(iii)   A special coach service from Britain to Grenoble, which operates during the summer months.

13.   West Mercia Insurance Services: High Street, Wombourne, near Wolverhampton WV5 9DN. Tel (0902) 892661. Specialists in holiday travel, mountaineering and mountain rescue insurance.

14.   Thomas Cook Group Ltd: P.O. Box 36, Thorpe Wood, Peterborough PE3 6SB. Tel (0733) 63200. Ask for details of their Independent Traveller Insurance Scheme.

15.   Club Alpin Français (CAF): 7 Rue La Boétie, Paris 75008. Members benefit from discounts at CAF refuges.

Printed by Carnmor Print & Design,
95/97, London Road, Preston, Lancashire.